Who Was Socrates?

By ALBAN D. WINSPEAR

UNIVERSITY OF WISCONSIN

and TOM SILVERBERG

The Cordon Company

Designed by Burnshaw

MANUFACTURED IN THE UNITED STATES OF AMERICA
SET UP, PRINTED, AND BOUND BY QUINN & BODEN COM-
PANY, INC., RAHWAY, NEW JERSEY

PREFACE

THE results of recent scholarship on the subject of Socrates seem to make more and more imperative a fresh interpretation of his baffling and enigmatical figure. In recent years there has been a marked tendency to deal with all the great ancient thinkers in terms of a consistent pattern of development in their thought and to see them not, as it were, full grown and maturely developed but in the slow process of growth and evolution. The genetic method has been applied to Plato with marked success by generations of scholars and has culminated in the monumental work of Lutoslawski. Prof. Werner Jaeger's book on Aristotle seems to me to establish quite clearly the validity of applying a similar method to Aristotle. It is not, therefore, surprising that a suggestion made as long ago as 1811 by Wolf in his edition of the *Clouds* should in recent years be revived and that there should be a fresh disposition to believe that the Socrates of the *Clouds* and the Socrates of the *Apology* represent quite different and in a sense even contradictory stages in his development as a thinker. As evidence for this tendency we need only cite the introduction to Mr. W. R. F. Hardie's *Study in Plato* (page 6). One of the most important contributions of Prof. A. E. Taylor to the understanding of Socrates was made in his *Varia Socratica*—the perception that the trial was closely bound up with the political strivings of the time.

But before an adequate explanation of the development of Socrates was possible, it was necessary to see much more clearly than has heretofore been possible, the relation of Socrates to the political struggles and social currents of his time. This could scarcely have been done until the ingenuity of a number of scholars had reconstructed the case for the prosecution as it was offered in

PREFACE

the lost pamphlet of Polycrates. This piece of reconstruction removes much of the problem of the relation of Socrates to the politics of his times from the realm of speculation to the realm of ascertained fact.

In addition to obligations noted at the proper time in footnotes, the authors feel conscious of a number of particular obligations. To Mr. William Kirsch and Miss Hildegard Pilger we owe the opportunity to consult the recent work done by the Russians on the subject of Greek philosophy. As if this debt were not already a sufficient one, Mr. Kirsch has read the work through in MSS. and has made one or two extremely penetrating suggestions. Prof. W. R. Agard has been unfailing in his interest and help and on several points has made important contributions. Mr. J. J. Lyons has read the work in MSS. and helped immeasurably in bringing clarity into our exposition. Mr. Edwin Minar has assisted with the proofs and made a number of valuable suggestions.

A research grant from the Special Research Fund of the Graduate School of the University of Wisconsin, though given for quite a different project, has in a sense made this work possible. When my studies in Spain were interrupted by the outbreak of the civil war, it was necessary to change my plans. The preliminary studies which culminated in this work were made in Paris at that time.

Last year, feeling that the possibilities of the genetic approach to Socrates and his relations to the life of his times had been by no means sufficiently explored, I suggested to Mr. Silverberg as a thesis subject the Socrates of the *Apology* and the Socrates of the *Clouds*. The results of his work coincided amazingly with my own developing convictions, and our collaboration has resulted in this little book.

A. D. WINSPEAR,
Madison, Wisconsin,
February, 1939.

FOREWORD

ANYONE who reflects on the picture of Socrates which Aristophanes gives in his magnificent satiric drama, the *Clouds*, and then proceeds to contrast it with the picture given by Plato and Xenophon (a picture and a concept which have subsequently become part of the cultural tradition of the Western world), must be conscious of a contradiction. The Socrates of the *Clouds* excites the fury and the contempt of the playwright. Socrates is regarded as a thoroughly subversive influence, a typical sophist, a man who strives to undermine all right and justice, who indulges in a kind of eristic verbal quibbling, a technique that enables its master to question any and all absolute authority. In Plato we have the picture of a high-minded, noble and detached intellect, a recluse concerned only with spiritual values, a man devoted to law even to the point of sacrificing his own life. The Platonic Socrates holds it his supreme task to discover and transmit to others a concept of divine and absolute law and authority. As a result of his high-minded quest, Socrates, in this tradition, excites the resentment of the vulgar, intolerant, Philistine mob of Athenian democrats. Pursuing inflexibly and unswervingly his high purpose, he walks with open eyes, with calm and unhurried tread to the final bourne of martyrdom. Typical of much that has been said and written in this tradition (a tradition, by the way, which has burgeoned brightly in the nineteenth century) is the following passage, ". . . inwardly there was the 'royal heart of innocence,' the high enthusiasm which has enabled so many to meet with cheerfulness a martyr's death, and the philosophic reason which entirely triumphed over the animal instincts, which saw things as a whole, and which counted the loss a gain."[1] As a result of this "interpretation" Socrates has come to occupy a position in the veneration of the ages second only, perhaps, to that of Jesus.

In this book we propose to demonstrate that such an interpreta-

[1] Footnotes which do not contribute to the actual course of the argument have been incorporated in a final section.

tion is, to say the least, partial and one-sided. It results from turning one's back on the more earthy aspects of the historical Socrates, and viewing him as a kind of disembodied mind. It results, too, from a tendency to regard Socrates as a symbol of the triumphant, deathless idea, the vehicle of thoughts that in their own day excited persecution and derision, but which have for their followers a universal and timeless value.

If we are to be serious about the study of Socrates, the contradiction between the Aristophanic representation and the Platonic idealization of him is inescapable. The solution of this contradiction will do much to reveal Socrates as an historical figure. And it may be possible, in so doing, to supplant the tenacious conception of Socrates as a diaphanous, disembodied "moral example" with a new concept of Socrates as a personality and a human being.

The more one examines the historical Socrates, the more uncertain one becomes of his value as a moral example. To point out weaknesses and flaws in the picture of rounded perfection that the ages have invented (with the competent assistance of Plato) has a value that far transcends any mere muck-raking for its own sake. It sheds light on the genesis of a type of thinking, a kind of *Weltanschauung,* which is even to this day subtly pervasive in the intellectual centers of the Western world. For in dealing with Socrates, we are dealing with the historic beginnings of idealism, both as a philosophy and a way of life. The appearance of Greek idealism as a systematic philosophy before Socrates is tenuous and controversial. In the Platonic Socrates and Plato himself we have traditional idealism as a fairly rounded and apparently coherent philosophy of life.

Our intention, then, is to examine the incidents which surround the birth of an important epoch in the history of thought. And if we tend to substitute for the philosophic Socrates a philodoxical Socrates, there should be gain rather than loss in the process; for while we shall be giving up a beautiful and compelling picture— which the nineteenth century made so emotionally poetic—we shall be drawing closer to a more prosaic truth, essentially more human and more real.

WHO WAS SOCRATES?

PART I

THE EARLY SOCRATES

SOCRATES emerged from a humble background. His parents were members of the rising class of skilled artisans who, in the period just ten years after the Persian Wars, were for the first time beginning to achieve prominence. It was this class, created by the new mercantilism, that in the fifth century was to provide the backbone for the brilliant Athenian democracy.

Socrates was born around the year 470 B C.[1] His mother, Phaenarete, is mentioned as a skilled midwife.[2] Whether she turned this skill to profit is not certain, but it is possible.

According to the long accepted tradition, his father, Sophroniscus, was a craftsman who exercised his art in sculpturing and stone cutting.[3] From this we get a hint immediately of Socrates' social position. In Greek antiquity the artist was not regarded with the same respect that the modern age accords him. Plutarch tells us that no well-born and well-endowed young man would want to be a Phidias or a Polycleitus. "Labor with one's hands on lowly tasks gives witness in the toil thus expended on useless things to one's own indifference to higher things."[4]

It is hardly necessary to use so late an authority as Plutarch. In the Phaedrus Plato describes the Souls who get only a partial grasp of truth. With a specious kind of mathematical accuracy, he places them in a hierarchical arrangement, giving the first and highest ranking to the philosopher and the second to the righteous king or warrior; the poet or other imitative artist is placed sixth; only the artisan or farmer, the sophist or demagogue, and the tyrant come lower in the scale. Plato represents the contemporary aristocratic point of view. Archimedes, who was perhaps the greatest practical engineering mind that antiquity produced, had this same prejudice so deeply ingrained that he turned his back on all practical studies, regarding every practical pursuit as ignoble and vulgar. According to Plutarch's account·

"And yet Archimedes possessed such a lofty spirit, so profound a soul, and such a wealth of scientific theory, that although his inventions had won for him a name and fame for super-human sagacity, he would not consent to leave behind him any treatise on this subject, but regarding the work of an engineer and every art that ministers to the needs of life as ignoble and vulgar, he devoted his efforts only to those studies, the subtlety and charm of which are not affected by the claims of necessity." [5]

There can be no question that in his early years Socrates followed the same useful and, to the Greeks, humble trade as his father. In fifth-century Greece there was a greater tendency for a son to follow in his father's footsteps, a tendency common in the early stages of the rise of a middle class. (The analogy of eighteenth-century France and early nineteenth-century England is striking.) Pausanias and Diogenes Laertius [6] speak of the three Graces on the Acropolis as the work of Socrates himself. The scholiast on Aristophanes' *Clouds* mentions the same tradition and says that they were in relief. Pausanias says that they were draped figures. Socrates playfully speaks of himself in the *Euthyphro* as a descendant of Daedalus, the legendary maker of wooden images.[7] There is thus a very well established tradition that Socrates had a hand in certain sculptures on the Acropolis. The fact that his work cannot be certainly identified with any extant remains means that popular tradition was too eager to make a concrete and dramatic association.

Some scholars argue that because Plato and Xenophon make no mention of Socrates' hardly reputable past, he cannot have been a stone cutter. But such an argument cannot be taken seriously. "He is depicted as always having had absolute leisure to occupy himself as his tastes directed and as having consorted from the first with the most distinguished men of Athens—the circles of Pericles and Cimon." [8] This is a clear misapprehension. It contradicts flatly the picture of Socrates and his ragged band of starving intellectuals given by Aristophanes in the *Clouds!* The root of Taylor's mis-conception seems quite clear in the following sentence: "Whether Sophroniscus was a statuary or not, we must not make the mistake of thinking of Socrates as belonging to a needy class like the modern 'proletariat.' " [9] Here lies a clear confusion in terms. There was nothing in ancient Athens at all analogous to the modern industrial proletariat. Sophroniscus was an artisan and as such a member of the dynamic, rising, radical class of fifth-century Athens. The attitude of patrician Athenians to this group is suffi-ciently shown by the passage from Plutarch quoted above; and it need hardly be demonstrated that Plato fully shared this preju-dice.[10] Plato and Xenophon were not anxious to make a hero of Aristophanes' vulgar, petty-bourgeois democrat. They were inter-ested, as we shall show, in the later Socrates, the martyred intellec-tual, victim (so they chose to believe) of the intolerance of his own kind. It was important for Plato and Xenophon to ignore or conceal his artisan past.

The argument that Sophroniscus seriously attempted to trace his lineage to Daedalus is almost too fantastic. Only very great gentlemen had leisure and opportunity for such luxuries as divine or semi-divine ancestors. It is much more plausible to think of Daedalus as a kind of guild or craft patron, like Homer for the poets and Aesculapius for physicians.

The supreme difficulty of this traditional explanation of Socrates as a man of leisure is that it completely fails to make sense of Aristophanes' play, the *Clouds.* It must treat as harmless fun what is clearly biting and malicious social satire, in a difficult war period, when the issues between oligarchy and democracy were heightened and exacerbated, when for the first time in many years the reverses suffered by the democratic war policy gave reaction its opportunity to loose a flood of criticism. Under such treatment Aristophanic satire suffers the extraction of its sting and, instead of a weapon of social reality, becomes a mere pointless and good-humored buffoonery. Taylor even suggests that the *Clouds* is to be taken simply in fun because in the *Symposium,* Socrates and Aristophanes are patently on terms of excellent good fellowship.[11]

It is worth remembering that according to an ancient tradition Plato found keen delight in the works of Aristophanes, they were found on his death bed and he is said to have composed the following epigram to the poet. 'The Graces seeking to find a shrine that should never perish, discovered the soul of Aristophanes.' Obviously Plato [born in 429 or 427] could not have known Aristophanes in 423 when relations between the poet and the 'Master' were somewhat embittered.

In other words, this theory assumes that because Socrates and Aristophanes are intimate in 416 they were also intimate in the period from 432-423 when this terrific attack on the democracy, its artists, its thinkers, its policy, was being prepared.

It involves the further false assumption that the argument between the "sophists" and their conservative or religious opponents was a purely abstract, intellectual discussion. The very reverse is true. The intellectual argument was closely bound up with the political argument. Anaxagoras, Phidias, Euripides, Socrates, all excited the anger of the oligarchs because their thinking and their creative achievements represented the intellectual and artistic side of the radical or democratic movement. The general lines of this intellectual attack on the conservative and theological tradition are very clear. In the fifth century it took the form which we describe as the sophistic movement. Sophistic thought became a systematic philosophy—a system in the sense that it developed formal precepts and *dicta*—with Protagoras and Gorgias. But developed sophistic philosophy of the fifth century emerged out of several historical tendencies which must be traced back at least to the period of Hesiod's poems.

It is important to notice at the start that the great sophists were chiefly interested in the problem of justice; what it is for individual man, and what it is in society.

It is most important for the student of philosophy to notice that it is just in this period, when the tribal order, with its close-knit interrelation of persons, is breaking up that the concept of the individual as opposed to society comes more and more into prominence. Greek literature from the Homeric poems to the fifth century is marked increasingly by a tendency to accentuate the 'spirit of individualism.' In sophistic philosophy the individual becomes an independent unit. Here we might notice by way of comparison the increasing importance of the individual in the development of Roman jurisprudence, as well as the growth of a similar spirit in the literature and thought of the Renaissance, as man began to free himself from feudal relations.

It is precisely this problem of justice which occupies a central position in the primitive, peasant outlook of Hesiod. The poet is uncomfortably aware that justice had fled from the earth. For this he blames the gift-devouring kings who give crooked judgments. Hesiod represents the dispossessed peasantry who were ground down by the landowning class as the tribal order decomposed (a process represented in its later stages by the Homeric poems), as inequality developed and the patrician state arose. The peasant complains of his hardships, hunger, indebtedness and cold, he complains of the injustice of his social superiors, the gift-devouring kings. His relations to them are like those of the nightingale to the hawk, borne aloft in his talons and complaining piteously. But he (the hawk) exclaims, "Wretch, why do you weep? A much stronger creature now has you in his power. You will go where I take you, well though you can sing. I shall make a meal of you if I wish or let you go. He is a fool who wants to contend with his betters!" [12] Hesiod is unable to understand what has come about as a result of social transformations. What he does see is that justice is no longer a set of rules that govern the interplay of equals in a highly coherent society. Hesiod, in a primitive and groping way, actually inaugurates the search for justice *outside* the framework of society. He is vaguely confident that an eternal principle of justice exists somewhere beyond the strife. The more the Hesiodic peasant suffers from injustice, bribery and crooked decisions, the more confident he is that justice will in the end prevail. In other words, with Hesiod, justice has begun its long ascent from earth to heaven. Interwoven with poetical imagery, Hesiod's own self-conscious realization is still struggling to bring into the clarity of explicit definition a concept that is still "felt" rather than thought. We might almost say that this is the birth of philosophy among the Greeks.

The social unrest which culminated in the reforms and concessions of Solon served to deepen and accentuate this interest in the nature of justice. For Solon the problem takes a different form. Justice for the first time in Western history becomes implicated with the state and its edicts. Solon was a liberal patrician,[18] forced to make concessions to the rising discontent of the dispossessed peasantry, but refusing to adopt the radical program of a cancellation of debts and a redivision of the land. He is at the same time the forerunner of the liberal mercantile movement, anticipating and interpreting its needs.

For Solon, injustice results from the avarice and greed of the wealthy [14]—"they have wealth through their following of unjust works and ways—neither the Sacred treasure nor that of the state do they spare in any wise, but they steal, each in his own corner, like men pillaging. They take no heed of the holy foundations of justice, who in silence marks what happens and what has been and who in course of time comes without fail to exact the penalty." The function of the legislator, and here Solon was thinking of himself, was to stand above the strife of classes and, to use his own image, hold a protective shield over each. "To the people I have given just as much power as suffices, neither taking away from their due nor offering more; while for those who had power and were honored for wealth I have taken thought likewise, that they should suffer nothing unseemly. I stand with strong shield flung around both parties, and have allowed neither to win an unjust victory." [15]

Here we find Solon developing two highly important ideas, which make their appearance for the first time in the history of Greek thought. Here, first, is the notion of justice as a principle involved in social relations, and, second, the earliest expression of a view that has since become widespread, that the state, in which justice is vested and with which it is identified, stands above and beyond the strife of particular interests.

Solon is, perhaps, the most germinal mind in early Greek thought, and we shall not be wrong in thinking of him not only as the father of Greek sophistic thought, but in a sense as the grandfather of political science and of all later philosophy. It is no accident that the Greeks thought of him as one of the seven great *sophoi*, or wise men; for from this concept of justice as embodied in human relations and realized in the state, stems both the critical and relativistic position of the sophists and the idealistic Platonic notion of the state as containing its own moral autonomy and as the reflection, here on earth, of the divine idea.

We may briefly touch on one further development of great importance. From Anaximander, the greatest and most mature of the Ionian physicists, we have a very interesting fragment preserved. It is short but pregnant with meaning: "They [i.e., the component elements of the physical world] make reparation and satisfaction to one another for their *injustice* as is appointed according to the ordering of time." (We prefer to translate "according to the ordered process of time.")[16]

It is difficult to see just what Burnet means by the 'ordering of time.' Does it mean that time is the subject and orders the process, or that time is the object and something else has established it in order? In either case what does it mean? *Taxin* seems to us to imply above all the notion of process. Burnet's translation obscures this.

The concept of justice as realized through the conflict of oppositions within the state, so explicitly developed by Solon, is transferred by this great Ionian to the cosmological oppositions which constitute the process of the natural world. Nothing could more clearly reveal than this fragment, when seen in its historical context, exactly how cosmological speculation developed among the

Greeks. And this is the first actual fragment preserved for us from the prose-writing philosophers of Greece.

We have here briefly outlined the two streams which reach their confluence in the widespread sophistic movement of the fifth century.

The sophists interested themselves in speculation about the nature of the physical universe.[17]

We are unable to understand Burnet's assertion, for which he gives no evidence, that the 'age of the Sophists is above all an age of reaction against science.' We much prefer the exposition offered by M. A. Dinnik in his 'Outlines of the History of Philosophy of Classical Greece,' ch. 7. 'One must especially mention the attack of Protagoras on Greek religion. It is this feature of his thought which sharply distinguishes him from Plato and marks his affinity with Democritus. This biographical detail about the historical Protagoras indicates the sharpness of the party conflict between science and religion in Ancient Greece. Protagoras was accused in Athens of atheism, a charge which necessarily carried with it the death sentence. As a result Protagoras was forced to flee Athens and at the time of crossing the sea he was drowned, his books were then publicly burned.'

The connection between Protagoras' ethical views and a scientific outlook is directly shown in a passage from Sextus Empiricus describing the philosophical position of this eminent sophist: 'What he states, then, is this—that matter is in flux, and as it flows additions are made continuously in the place of the effluxions, and the senses are transformed and altered according to the times of and to all the other conditions of the bodies. He says also that the "reasons" of all the appearances subsist in matter, so that matter, so far as it depends on itself, is capable of being all those things which appear to all. And men, he says, apprehend different things at different times owing to their differing dispositions; for he who is in a natural state apprehends those things subsisting in matter which are able to appear to those in a natural state, and those who are in a non-natural state the things which can appear to those in a non-natural state. Moreover, precisely the same account applies to the variations due to age, and to the sleeping or waking state, and to each several kind of condition. Thus according to him, Man becomes the criterion of real existences, for all things that appear to men also exist, and things that appear to no man have no existence either.'

This occupation, this interest in physical speculation, one might think to be harmless enough. But to think this is to fail to see the danger. Physical speculation, as we have seen, arose out of an interest in the meaning and nature of justice. In the fifth century this association continued. For physical speculation, in this period, brought with it ethical and social skepticism; threatening to undo the very foundations on which the conservative position was founded. Instead of seeing in the traditional Athenian state a reflection of the divine idea, an affirmation of its own moral autonomy, a claim to the unquestioning obedience of possessing and dispossessed alike, the radical thinkers boldly proclaimed an ethical relativism; that man is the measure of all things, that (in the words of Thrasymachus) justice—the whole nexus of constitutional law and popular custom, of juridical arrangement and parliamentary decree, is the interest of the class in power (the stronger). that an oligarchy when in power legislates in its interest, a tyrant in his interest, a democracy in its interest. Here, too, is the genesis of the *nomos-physis* argument. Whereas the conservatives wanted to make of justice and statute-law something inherent in the very nature of things and worthy, therefore, of unquestioning acceptance and obedience, the sophists wished to make justice a matter of convention, of arbitrary external pressure; so that when custom comes into conflict with "natural laws" and "human nature" then custom must give way. Such doctrines were clearly skeptical, subversive and revolutionary. And it is no wonder that they stirred up the hatred, suspicion, fury and contempt of the conservative and oligarchical class.

So far we can characterize the sophistic movement as a whole.

But it is important to make further distinctions and to indicate a diversity within sophistic tendencies. We may illustrate our point by contrasting two important sophists. Protagoras is a pure relativist. "Man is the measure of all things." No human institution, therefore, can claim absolute validity or correspondence to anything ultimately real. For him a concept applies solely to the subjective side. In other words, reality is an interpretation rather than a "thing in itself." Thrasymachus, too, is a relativist, but there is one highly important difference; his relativism is objective rather than subjective. In other words, for him justice is relative to the interest of the dominant class: it is, however, a positive and objective thing, although considered in the totality of the process—that is, genetically and historically—relative and transient. The position of Protagoras is ambiguous and bivalent: although in its incidence liberal and critical of a *status quo,* by its denial of *all* objective validity to the concept, by its insistence on a universal flexibility of judgment, it can equally well be used as a weapon of conservatism. To put it more concretely, by Protagorean standards the claim of the oligarchical state to the unquestioning obedience of its subjects can have no objective justification. But equally, the right of the democrats to overthrow the oligarchical state can find no substantiation in any real and objective order. The insistence of Thrasymachus that justice is the tangible domination in wealth and political power of one group over another makes of justice a thing which can be observed and studied in its relative changing forms. It is no accident, therefore, that the conservative Plato, in his greatest work, makes Thrasymachus the supreme enemy. Plato was very well aware of the difference between Thrasymachus and Protagoras. It is no accident that, while he speaks of Protagoras with a certain amount of respect, when he comes to the final "refutation" of Thrasymachus in *The Republic* he stresses the view that the real sophist is the mob.

"Do you really think, as people so often say, that our youth are corrupted by Sophists, or that private teachers of the art corrupt them in any degree worth speaking of? Are not the public who say these things the greatest of all Sophists? And do they not educate to perfection young and old, men and women alike, and fashion them after their own hearts?

"When is this accomplished? he said.

"When they meet together, and the world sits down at an assembly, or in a court of law, or a theater, or a camp, or in any other popular resort, and there is a great uproar, and they praise some things which are being said or done, and blame other things, equally exaggerating both, shouting and clapping their hands, and the echo of the rocks and the place in which they are assembled redoubles the sound of the praise or blame—at such a time will not a young man's heart, as they say, leap within him? Will any private training enable him to stand firm against the overwhelming flood of popular opinion? or will he be carried away by the stream? Will he not have the notions of good and evil which the public in general have—he will do as they do, and as they are, such will he be?

"Yes, Socrates; necessity will compel him.

"And yet, I said, there is a still greater necessity, which has not been mentioned.

"What is that?

"The gentle force of attainder or confiscation or death, which, as you are aware, these new Sophists and educators, who are the public, apply when their words are powerless.

"Indeed they do; and in right good earnest.

"Now what opinion of any other Sophist, or of any private person, can be expected to overcome in such an unequal contest?

"None, he replied.

"No, indeed, I said, even to make the attempt is a great piece of folly; there neither is, nor has been, nor is ever likely to be, any different type of character which has had no other training in virtue but that which is supplied by public opinion—I speak, my friend, of human virtue only, what is more than human, as the proverb says, is not included: for I would not have you ignorant that, in the present evil state of governments, whatever is saved and comes to good is saved by the power of God, as we may truly say.

"I quite assent, he replied.

"Then let me crave your assent to a further observation.

"What are you going to say?

"Why, that all those mercenary individuals, whom the many call Sophists and whom they deem to be their adversaries, do, in fact, teach nothing but the opinion of the many, that is to say, the opinions of their assemblies; and this is their wisdom. I might compare them to a man who should study the tempers and desires of a mighty strong beast who is fed by him—he would learn how to approach and handle him, also at what times and from what causes he is dangerous or the reverse, and what is the meaning of his several cries, and by what sounds, when another utters them, he is soothed or infuriated; and you may suppose further, that when, by continually attending upon him, he has become perfect in all this, he calls his knowledge wisdom, and makes of it a system or art, which he proceeds to teach, although he has no real notion of what he means by the principles or passions of which he is speaking, but calls this honorable and that dishonorable, or good or evil, or just or unjust, all in accordance with the tastes and tempers of the great brute. Good he pronounces to be that in which the beast delights and evil to be that which he dislikes; and he can give no other account of them except that the just and noble are the necessary, having never himself seen, and having no power of explaining to others the nature of either, or the difference between them, which is immense. By heaven, would not such an one be a rare educator?

"Indeed he would.

"And in what way does he who thinks that wisdom is the discernment of the tempers and tastes of the motley multitude, whether in painting or music, or, finally, in politics, differ from him whom I have been describing? For when a man consorts with the many, and exhibits to them his poem or other work of art or the service which he has done the State, making them his judges when he is not obliged, the so-called necessity of Diomede will oblige him to produce whatever they praise. And yet the reasons are utterly ludicrous which they give in confirmation of their own notions about the honorable and good. Did you ever hear any of them which were not?" [18]

Two things are very apparent in this passage—Plato's furious dislike for democracy and democratic procedure, and the identification in his mind of sophistic thinking and the democracy.

To complete the picture, we should see how the relativism of Protagoras can be developed into a defense of strong-arm methods, and a rationalization of social inequalities. Its very denial of objective values can be interpreted in such a way that there is no reason for rejecting and opposing injustice. So from the neutral or centrist position of Protagoras in regard to the problem of justice, evolved historically both the radical objective skepticism of Thrasymachus, and the doctrines of a group of anti-democratic sophists like Polus, Callicles,[19] Crito and Hippodamus who carried on the same doctrine to its final implications on the subjective side.

The implication of Callicles' doctrine, his defense of the strong man is clearly anti-democratic, although Plato who distrusts all shades of relativism, for the purpose of opposing him, represents him as still a democrat.

This last position can best be summed up in the luminous phrases of Callicles in the *Gorgias:*

"This is that which is by nature fair and just; the man who is to live aright ought to permit his desires to become as great as possible and not to check them; and when the desires have grown to their fullest extent he should be able to gratify them because of his courage and intelligence." [20]

Now it is quite clear from all that we know of the early Socrates that the young artisan, the stone cutter, son of a stone cutter and a midwife, a typical representative of the rising artisan class, was deeply influenced by the democratic currents which were stirring the intellectual life of the fifth century. Plato's description of Socrates' early interests is particularly significant. "He began," says Plato,[21] "with a great curiosity for research into nature and an eagerness to unearth the causes of the coming of things into being and their passing away." The impulse to critical philosophy was social and political; the coming into being of the democracy and the passing away of the oligarchy. Change and process had become the most important concepts, and philosophy was turning to the physical world where the laws of change and development were embodied. Socrates was one of the young intellectuals who lived through the experience of at least part of this revolutionary period. The impact of tremendous social change gave a scientific direction to his thought.

The philosopher Anaxagoras brought into focus and gave utterance to the dominant progressive tendencies of middle-class Athenian thought in the second half of the fifth century. To understand this point it is necessary to go back a little and show the development of social relations in fifth-century Athens.

The late tribal order represented in the Homeric poems broke up in the eighth and seventh centuries, B C. This breakup was a direct result of a change in the economic organization of the Greek world. It grew out of advancing agricultural techniques, out of production for a market and the rise of a monetary economy, with the consequent development of usury and the mortgage, out of usury and speculation developed social and economic inequality, a class of landed proprietors on the one hand, and of needy and even dispossessed peasants on the other. The tribal order was succeeded by the aristocratic state, a dictatorship of a small group of great families, the *Eupatrids,* or landed proprietors. The dominance of this class found political expression in the court of the Areopagus. The same movement which led to the breakup of the tribal order led to the development of another powerful interest in the state—the mercantile or democratic group, whose interests were served by imperialism and trade.

To avoid any possible confusion, our use of the term 'imperialism' ought to be clarified. We do not intend to suggest that ancient imperialism shares the same characteristics and dynamics as nineteenth-century capitalism or modern imperialism. Ancient 'imperialism' was based on the need to control sources of food supply; and to a lesser degree to control the market for the products of intensive agriculture and primitive crafts. In addition it was based on the need for constant expansion in order to keep up the supply of slaves on which the entire productive system was founded, although this last characteristic is probably more evident in the Roman Empire than the Greek city state.

The social struggles of the sixth and early fifth century turned on the opposition, in the slave-owning Athenian polity, between the landed proprietors, or oligarchs and the traders, merchants, speculators and artisans. The oligarchs, who were, after all, a small minority numerically, tended to look for support to Sparta, the most conservative and oligarchical of Greek fifth-century cities. But the democrats tended in the early stages, until their own developing imperialism brought them sharply into conflict with Persia, to look to the Great King for a counterbalance to Spartan influence. As late as Marathon, while the democrats were still intriguing with Persia, the oligarchs could come forward as the patriotic party. Under Miltiades they did so. In the sixth century and through the greater part of the fifth, the democratic movement was led by liberal patricians like Solon and the great Alcmaeonid family. There seems no good ground for rejecting the suspicion that the Alcmaeonids were the party in Athens who, in conjunction with Hippias, were prepared to open the gates of Athens to the Persian invader [22] and signaled their willingness by raising the shield from Mt. Pentelicus.

But by the outbreak of the Peloponnesian War the balance of forces had shifted very considerably. The policy of Pericles, representing as it did the interests of the large slave-owning business group, was relatively moderate. But now a "left wing" group was pressing hard upon the more moderate democrats. The growth of slave production, of trade, of money capital as well as the growth of a "lumpen proletariat," who parasitically lived off the bounty of imperialism, led to strong pressure for a more aggressive foreign policy, for a more intoxicating imperial idea. The bankers, speculators, petty artisans, wheat traders and "lumpen proletariat" all united to form a strong pressure group that called for more aggressiveness in foreign affairs and a more generous distribution of loot in the form of increased payment for state services. This union led to the short-lived ascendancy of Cleon and became even more boisterous, vehement, and articulate under his successor, Hyperbolus. The position of Pericles became more and more uneasy. "Now Pericles became another," says Plutarch. "He was no longer an obedient tool in the hands of the people, not so readily did he yield in accordance with the demands of the throng." [23] In the earlier part of his ascendancy it was Thucydides * and his oligarchs who led the attack on Pericles. At the time of the outbreak of the Peloponnesian War, he seems so much under attack from both sides that Diogenes Laertius [24] is uncertain whether the attack on Anaxagoras, the outstanding philosopher of Periclean democracy, was led by Thucydides or Cleon. He mentions both traditions. [25]

The resolution of this particular difficulty depends, of course, on the view one takes of the date of the trial of Anaxagoras. If we follow Taylor and place the trial around 450, then Thucydides, who was, as Plutarch tells us, a leader of the party of the good and true [i.e., the Oligarchs] must have preferred the accusation; for this is too early for Cleon. However, if we choose the accepted date, around 432, Cleon is the more probable nominee. A further example of this confusion is provided by Diopeithes. On the basis of a line in the *Birds* [988] Burnet [p. 296] assumes that he was a democrat, and adds an extraordinary footnote: 'Aristophanes had no respect for orthodoxy when combined with democratic opinions.' It is by no means certain that he was a democrat.

Seldom in history do we find the same transparent unity of ideas and social struggles that we find in fifth-century Greece. Indeed, thought always is consciously or unconsciously a reflection of social forces, but in the Greek world the connection is particu-

* The son of Melesias. not the historian, Thucydides.

larly vivid. In the fifth century, the struggle between oligarchs and democrats found its reflection in the mental and artistic argument between the conservative, theological, idealistic tradition, and its naturalistic, relativistic and skeptical critics. Of the one tendency Sophocles will provide an apt example; of the other, Euripides.

Corresponding exactly to the ambiguous position of Pericles in the struggles of Athenian politics in the last two decades before the Peloponnesian War was the theoretical system of Anaxagoras, the philosopher of the Periclean age. Only by seeing the relation of the thinking of Socrates to that of Anaxagoras, can the mind of Socrates be understood.

The political world at Athens convinced Anaxagoras that change was ruthlessly real and that the security of any institution or class, perhaps even the Periclean democracy, was only relative to the tides of human progress and might be swept away in the inevitable process of things. The democracy had vanquished the oligarchy, but how long could the democracy of Pericles itself endure? It was just as frail and temporary as any other institution, and institutions, like plants and animals, were part of the great cycle of creation and destruction. Had man's social life no other security than an endless series of transformations? As Anaxagoras contemplated the political world of democratic Athens he must have been struck by an arresting phenomenon, how the cool, aloof, Olympian mind of Pericles dominated the chaos and the confusion, just as the city of the maiden Athena, Athena type of the divine wisdom, born in full panoply and complete maturity from the very mind of Zeus, could order the chaos of Aegean politics. And just as the political position of Pericles was ambiguous and paradoxical, a blend of the progressive and the static, so two opposite movements manifest themselves in the thinking of his friend Anaxagoras. On the one hand there is the consciousness of change and process, of mixture and separation. "The Hellenes," he says, "follow a wrong usage in speaking of coming into being and passing away, for nothing comes into being or passes away, but there is mingling and separation of things that are. So they would be right to call coming into being, mixture and passing away, separation." [26]

"Things revolve and are separated out by force and swiftness. And the swiftness makes the force. Their swiftness is not like the swiftness of any of the things that are now among men, but in every way many times as swift."

This aspect of his thinking manifests itself in a curiosity about physical phenomena, research into mechanical, biological and physiological change. "How can hair come from what is not hair or flesh from not flesh?" [27]

". . . We must suppose that there are contained many things and all sorts in the things that are uniting, seeds of all things, with all sorts of shapes and colors and savors, and that men have been formed in them and the other animals that have life, and that these men have inhabited cities and cultivated fields as with us, and that there are the sun and the moon and the rest, as with us." [28]

"But before they were separated off, when all things were together not even was any color distinguishable, for the mixture of all things prevented it; of the moist and the dry, and the warm and the cold and the light and the dark and of much earth that was in it and of a multitude of innumerable seeds in no other way like each other. For none of the other things either is like any other; and these things being so we must hold that all things are in the whole." [29]

"The things that are in the world are not divided nor cut off from one another with a hatchet, neither the warm from the cold, nor the cold from the warm." [30]

"With the rise of the dog star men begin the harvest, with its setting they begin to till the fields. It is hidden for forty days and nights." [31]

These quotations make clear the interest of Anaxagoras in physical process. He is acutely aware of the Heraclitean doctrine of the flux. They reveal, too, that he is fully conscious of the Heraclitean view of the "tension of opposites." In Anaxagoras and Heraclitus we have a kind of naive foreshadowing of the Hegelian doctrine of the "interpenetration of opposites." For these thinkers, as for Hegel, creation and destruction were the result of the strife of opposites and their interpenetration. This is the significance of Anaxagoras' metaphor of the hatchet. "It is of those opposites," writes Burnet of Anaxagoras, "and not of the different forms of matter that everything contains a portion. Every particle, however large or however small, contains every one of those opposite qualities; that which is hot is also to a certain extent cold. Even snow Anaxagoras affirmed was black, that is even the white contains a certain portion of the opposite quality. It is enough to indicate the connection of this with the views of Heraclitus." [82] In support of this position, it will be sufficient to quote just one fragment from Heraclitus—"We must know that war is common to all and *strife is justice,* and that all things come into being and pass away through strife." [83]

One side of Anaxagoras, therefore, expressed the most vigorous radical skepticism. It embodied the scientific curiosity of the materialists who carried into philosophy the enquiring spirit of the new democracy. Unhesitatingly it sought for rational explanations of all physical phenomena in terms of structure and causality. As far as science was concerned, Anaxagoras carried on the tradition of the Ionic school whose researches and speculations dealt largely with tangible reality and natural causes.

The other side of his thinking, however, presents a sharp contrast to the materialist cosmology and in fact clearly represents a retreat from materialism and science. A world composed of bodily existence and process was not, for the reason we have indicated, enough to satisfy Anaxagoras. At this point he departed completely from previous physical philosophies by introducing the agency of *Nous,* or mind, as the center of integration and order in the universe and as one stable principle which is unaffected by the laws of change.

"All other things partake in a portion of everything, while *Nous* is infinite and self-ruled, and is mixed with nothing, but is alone, itself by itself. For if it were not by itself, but were mixed with anything else, it would partake in all things if it were mixed with any, for in everything there is a portion of everything, as has been said by me in what goes before, and the things mixed with it would hinder it, so that it would have power over nothing in the same way that it has now being alone by itself. For it is the thinnest of all things and the purest, and it has all knowledge about everything and the greatest strength; and *Nous* has power over all things, both greater and smaller, that have life. And *Nous* had power over the whole revolution, so that it began to revolve in the beginning. And it began to revolve first from a small beginning; but the revolution now extends over a larger space, and will extend over a larger still. And all the things that are mingled together and separated off and distinguished are all known by *Nous*. And *Nous* set in order all things that were to be, and all things that were and are not now and that are, and this revolution in which now revolve the stars and the sun and the moon, and the air and the aether that are separated off. And this revolution caused the separating off, and the rare is separated off from the dense, the warm from the cold, the light from the dark, and the dry from the moist. And there are many portions in many things. But nothing is altogether separated off nor distinguished from anything else except *Nous*. And all *Nous* is alike, both the greater and the smaller; while nothing else is like anything else, but each single thing is and was most manifestly those things of which it has most in it." [34]

"And when *Nous* began to move things, separating off took place from all that was moved, and so far as *Nous* set in motion all was separated. And as things were set in motion and separated, the revolution caused them to be separated much more." [35]

"And *Nous*, which ever is, is certainly there, where everything else is, in the surrounding mass and in what has been united with it and separated off from it." [36]

Despite the fact that Anaxagoras introduced *Nous* as a first principle he was by no means setting up a real antithesis between matter and spirit. This is quite clear from the passage in the *Phaedo*, discussed more fully below, in which Socrates expresses his disappointment with the account which Anaxagoras gives of the function of *Nous* in the universe.

For Anaxagoras the problem was to reconcile the struggle that went on in his own mind, the contradiction between his knowledge of a purely physical universe and his feeling that a permanent reality must lie behind the world to order and control it. Anaxagoras never succeeded in fully harmonizing these two discordant aspects of his own thinking. There is on the one hand the world of flux, there is on the other *Nous*, arranging and ordering. His solution is in the last analysis a juxtaposition rather than a synthesis. For synthesis was impossible to a man caught, as was any member of Pericles' circle, in the ambiguities of Pericles' social and political position. He could not disregard the fact of change, for that would have been absurd. But change loomed large and terrifying. The men around Pericles were vaguely conscious of forces beyond their own limited control and from this terrifying prospect they recoiled in horror; they felt an unconscious urge to find some principle of permanence that would give meaning to the transitory and the evanescent. The psychology implied in this search for the permanent, the unchanging, the authoritative has never been better displayed than in Browning's poem, *Abt Vogler*.

Well, it is gone at last, the palace of music I reared;
Gone! and the good tears start, the praises that come too slow;
For one is assured at first, one scarce can say that he feared,
That he even gave it a thought, the gone thing was to go.
Never to be again! but many more of the kind
As good, nay, better perchance· is this your comfort to me?
To me, who must be saved because I cling with my mind
To the same, same self, same love, same God aye, what was
     shall be.

Therefore to whom turn I but to Thee, the ineffable Name?
Builder and maker, Thou, of houses not made with hands!
What, have fear of change from Thee who art ever the same?
Doubt that Thy power can fill the heart that Thy power expands?

There shall never be one lost good! What was, shall live as before;
The evil is null, is nought, is silence implying sound;
What was good, shall be good, with, for evil, so much good more;
On the earth the broken arcs; in the heaven, a perfect round.

We have discussed the socio-psychological process presented by
the enigmatic figure of Anaxagoras because only in the light of
this process can the mind of Socrates be explored.

Nothing is better established in our tradition than the fact that
Socrates experienced a philosophical conversion. Plato gives a full
account of the process in the *Phaedo*. This passage is so important
that we quote it in full.

"Then I will tell you, said Socrates. When I was young, Cebes,
I had a prodigious desire to know that department of philosophy
which is called the investigation of nature; to know the causes of
things and why a thing is and is created or destroyed appeared
to me to be a lofty profession; and I was always agitating myself
with the consideration of questions such as these:—Is the growth
of animals the result of some decay which the hot and cold principle contracts, as some have said? Is the blood the element with
which we think, or the air, or the fire? or perhaps nothing of the
kind—but the brain may be the originating power of the percep-
tions of hearing and sight and smell, and memory and opinion
may come from them, and science may be based on memory and
opinion when they have attained fixity. And then I went on to
examine the corruption of them, and then to the things of heaven
and earth, and at last I concluded myself to be utterly and absolutely incapable of these enquiries, as I will satisfactorily prove
to you. For I was fascinated by them to such a degree that my
eyes grew blind to things which I had seemed to myself, and also
to others, to know quite well; I forgot what I had before thought
self-evident truths; e.g., such a fact as that the growth of man is
the result of eating and drinking; for when by the digestion of
food flesh is added to flesh and bone to bone, and whenever there
is an aggregation of congenial elements, the lesser bulk becomes
larger and the small man great."

". . . Then I heard someone reading, as he said, from a book of Anaxagoras, that mind was the disposer and cause of all, and I was delighted at this notion, which appeared quite admirable and I said to myself. If mind is the disposer, mind will dispose all for the best, and put each particular in the best place; and I argued that if anyone desired to find out the cause of the generation or state of being or doing or suffering was best for that thing, and therefore a man had only to consider the best for himself and others and then he would also know the worse, since the same science comprehended both. And I rejoiced to think that I had found in Anaxagoras a teacher of the causes of existence such as I desired, and I imagined that he would tell me first whether the earth is flat or round, and whichever was true, he would proceed to explain the cause and the necessity of this being so, and then he would teach me the nature of the best and show that this was best; and if he said that the earth was in the centre, he would further explain that this position was the best, and I should be satisfied with the explanation given, and not want any other sort of cause. And I thought that I would then go on and ask him about the sun and moon and stars, and that he would explain to me their comparative swiftness, and their returnings and various states, active and passive, and how all of them were for the best. For I could not imagine that when he spoke of mind as the disposer of them, he would give any other account of their being as they are, except that this was best; and I thought that when he had explained to me in detail the cause of each and cause of all, he would go on to explain to me what was best for each and what was good for all. These hopes I would not have sold for a large sum of money, and I seized the books and read them as fast as I could in my eagerness to know the better and the worse.

"What expectations I had formed, and how grievously was I disappointed! As I proceeded, I found my philosopher altogether forsaking mind or any other principle of order, but having recourse to air, and ether, and water, and other eccentricities. I might compare him to a person who began by maintaining generally that mind is the cause of the actions of Socrates, but who, when he endeavored to explain the causes of my several actions in detail, went on to show that I sit here because my body is made up of bones and muscles, and the bones, as he would say, are hard and have joints which divide them, and the muscles are elastic, and they cover the bones, which have also a covering or environment of flesh and skin which contains them; and as the bones are lifted at their joints by the contraction or relaxation of the muscles, I am able to bend my limbs, and this is why I am sitting here in a curved posture—that is what he would say; and he would have a similar explanation of my talking to you, which he would attribute to sound, and air, and hearing, and he would assign ten thousand other causes, which is, that the Athenians have thought fit to condemn me, and accordingly I have thought it better and more right to remain here and undergo my sentence, for I am inclined to think that these muscles and bones of mine would have gone off long ago to Megara or Boeotia—by the dog they would, if they had been only by their own idea of what was best, and if I had not chosen the *better* and *nobler* part, instead of playing truant and running away, of enduring any punishment which the *state* inflicts. There is surely a strange confusion of causes and conditions in all this. It may be said, indeed, that without bones and muscles and the other parts of the body I cannot execute my purposes. But to say that I do as I do because of them, and that this is the way in which mind acts, and not from the choice of the best, is a very careless and idle mode of speaking. I wonder that they cannot distinguish the cause from the condition, which the many, feeling about in the dark, are always mistaking and misnaming. And thus one man makes a vortex all round and steadies the earth by the heaven, another gives the air as a support to the earth, which is a sort of broad trough. Any power which in arranging them as they are arranges them for the best never enters into their minds, and instead of finding any superior strength in it, they rather expect to discover another Atlas of the world who is stronger and more everlasting and more containing than the good,—of the obligatory and containing power of the good they think nothing, and yet this is the principle which I would fain learn if anyone would teach me." [37]

Xenophon, whose mind was far less subtle, but whose capacity for hero worship was certainly as great, lets slip one or two hints about Socrates' early enthusiasms that tend to support Plato's account. He tells us that Socrates' school at one stage in his career had consisted of a group of scientific investigators, [38] that he possessed advanced knowledge of astronomy and geometry. [39] There is a certain naiveté about Xenophon's description of Socrates' contact with natural science. In the *Memorabilia* he states categorically, at the start, that Socrates despised the investigations of scientists. "In the first place, he would enquire," reports Xenophon, "did these thinkers suppose that their knowledge of human affairs was so complete that they must seek these new fields for the exercise of their brains. . . ." [40] And again, "Indeed he would argue that to trouble one's mind with such problems was sheer folly." [41] Later on he seems to forget himself and tells us a number of startlingly contradictory things about his hero. "For instance, he said that the study of geometry should be pursued until the student was competent to measure a parcel of land accurately in case he wanted to take over, convey or divide it, or to compute the yield; and this knowledge was so easy to acquire, that anyone who gave his mind to mensuration knew the size of the piece and carried away a knowledge of the principles of land measurement. He was against carrying the study of geometry so far as to include the more complicated figures, on the ground that he could not see the use of them. Not that he was himself unfamiliar with them, but he said that they were enough to occupy a lifetime, to the complete exclusion of many other useful studies.

"Similarly he recommended them to make themselves familiar with astronomy, but only so far as to be able to find the time of night, month and year, in order to use reliable evidence when planning a journey by land or sea, or setting the watch, and in all other affairs that are done in the night or month or year, by distinguishing the times and seasons aforesaid." [42]

From the passage in the *Phaedo* just quoted one or two points arise in fairly clear outline. Socrates went through a philosophical conversion; this conversion was a turning-away from materialism and a concept of material causation to idealism and a belief in teleological causation. The transition came as a result of reading a book of Anaxagoras who had promised to exhibit "mind" as the ordering principle of the universe· He rejoiced if the book could really explain all process as well as all existence by showing what it was *best* that it should be. But he found to his great disappointment that Anaxagoras had not really synthesized mind and matter nor brought into harmony the concepts of mechanical and ideal causation. And finally this new way of thinking is represented by Plato as a sudden change, a revulsion of feeling due to his disappointment with the inadequacy of Anaxagoras' use of the concept of mind. Taylor's comment on the passage is as follows: "Of course since he gives us no chronological indications except that the events belong to the early life of Socrates, it is quite possible that the intellectual revolution he describes in a page or two may have taken some considerable time for its completion." [43] There is no need to be so agnostic on this point as Taylor. In the first place, it is antecedently highly improbable that a mind should make this kind of *volte face* and pass from materialism to idealism, as it were, overnight. In the second place, we have a great deal of positive evidence to demonstrate that Plato's account cannot be taken as a reliable story of Socrates' intellectual transition. From Theophrastus, an unusually reliable authority, who may himself have studied in the Academy (he was certainly in Athens during Plato's lifetime) but who turned away from idealism to botanical and biological investigations and had therefore no interest in re-creating a Platonic Socrates, we have the positive assertion that Socrates was a pupil of Archelaus, the successor of Anaxagoras as head of the school when the latter was forced to leave Athens. [44] Aristoxenus of Tarentum, an associate of Aristotle, says that Socrates was first introduced to Archelaus when he (Socrates) was seventeen and that their friendship continued for many years. [45] Diogenes Laertius preserves the remark of a fifth-century tragic poet, Ion of Chios, that Socrates, when a young man, visited the

island of Samos in the company of Archelaus. We can probably
attribute this visit to the year 441-40 when Athens was blockading
the island of Samos. Archelaus and Socrates, both young men
at the time, may have been serving in the Athenian force.

There is some evidence that the relationship between Archelaus
and his promising pupil was more intimate than modern taste
approves between a teacher and pupil. 'Diogenes Laertius says
that Socrates, when a boy, had been the favorite of his teacher
Archelaus, which is confirmed by Porphyrius, who says that
Socrates when a youth of seventeen years was not averse from
the love of Archelaus, for at that time he was much given to
sensuality, which was later supplanted by zealous intellectual
work.' [46]

Putting these statements together we get a fairly coherent picture. Socrates evidently spent many years in close association with
Archelaus and was probably a member of his school. [47]

Diogenes Laertius mentions as authorities Io, Aristoxenus, and
Diocles—a tradition going back to Socrates himself. Others who
mention this tradition are Cicero, Sextus, Porphyrius, Clement of
Alexandria, Simplicius, Eusebius, and Origen. Zeller has expressed
his disbelief in the association. His first argument to the contrary
is based on the silence of Plato, Xenophon and Aristotle. Certainly
the first two of these had good reasons for passing over lightly the
earlier materialistic and democratic associations of Socrates. Secondly, according to Zeller, Socrates refers to himself (in Xen.
Sym) as an *autourgos,* a self-taught philosopher. This weak denial
must be taken to refer to the later idealistic Socrates. Socrates
could well claim that in developing his idealistic point of view
he was an originator. But he never himself denied that he learned
from Anaxagoras. In his argument Zeller makes one more extraordinary assumption—that Socrates was seventeen years old when
Anaxagoras left Athens, and that at seventeen he must have

passed the stage of pupillage. That would reveal a remarkable precocity!

Nothing is known from contemporaries of the views of Archelaus —the comments concerning his actual philosophic opinions are those of much later authorities. The lack of firsthand information, however, is compensated by the unanimity of the doxographers on certain important points. From their isolated statements we can at least discern the basis for a tradition about the school of Archelaus It is very clear that he developed the philosophy of Anaxagoras in a materialistic direction.

Diogenes Laertius says [48] that he was the *first* to bring Ionian physical philosophy to Athens and was called a physicist. While this is clearly a mistake, it is an understandable mistake if Archelaus developed the materialistic side of Anaxagoras. Further, says Diogenes, "Physical philosophy ceased with him, for Socrates introduced 'ethics' "

Origen gives us a statement that is terse but arresting, Archelaus held that in mind subsists a kind of immediate mixture.[49] Stobaeus supports this view by attributing to Archelaus the statement that air is mind and God, but that mind is not a creative principle in the universe.[50]

Plutarch and others maintain that he regarded air as the first principle of things, and held that air and what was created from air by the process of condensation and rarefaction (water and fire) were infinite.[51]

"He treated the mixture of matter just as Anaxagoras had done and he treated first principles in the same way. He held that in mind subsists a kind of immediate mixture. The principle of motion lay in the separation from one another of heat and cold, that heat set things in motion and cold puts them at rest." So far his views make little advance on the physical theories of the Ionian school, in fact, his view of the separation of opposites and their strife as the ultimate causative principle is very close to Ionian doctrines. But in discussing the development of living creatures and

the evolution of man, Archelaus takes over the ideas of Anaximander and adds a new richness of content and description.
Anaximander had put in a somewhat obscure way the notions
that men were born "in the inside of fishes" and that "man was
like another animal, namely, a fish, in the beginning." But he
had seen, with remarkable insight, that human beings must have
emerged through an evolutionary development.[52] Archelaus, developing this theory, says that "as regards living creatures when the
earth grew warm, at first in its lower portion, wherever the warm
and the cold mingled, man appeared and many other living
creatures, all having the same mode of life, nurtured as they were
from the slime. The time required was not long—but later they
were begotten from each other. And men were separated off from
the others and established leaders and laws and arts and cities,
and so on. And he says that mind is developed in all living
creatures. Each uses intelligence, but some more slowly and some
more quickly." [53]

The most striking bit of information about Archelaus' thinking comes to us from Diogenes,[54] who makes it clear that Archelaus united his materialistic and evolutionary theories with a thoroughly sophistic view of ethics and human institutions "The just
and the base are not so by *nature* but rather by *convention*." There
could be no more convincing example of the inherent unity of
physical science and sophistic relativism.

We are now in a position to reconstruct something of the development of Socrates as a person and as a thinker in this early
period. We know that he began life in a very humble stratum of
society as a free artisan or even as a slave.[55]

This latter point cannot be pressed too far. Duris, in a tradition preserved by Diogenes Laertius, II, 19, represents him as a
slave. There is nothing inherently improbable in this conjecture.
We know from Thucydides that the great majority of the slaves
who deserted during the Peloponnesian War were *cheirotechnai*,
or craftsmen. We know that in building the Erechtheon in 409-8,

of those employed 28% were free men as opposed to 72% metics and slaves. The proportion would not be as high in the early part of the century, but the balance of probability is, on the face of it, still strong. Socrates was certainly not a metic.

He seems to have married a woman of his own class, Xanthippe, at an early age. Later he married a lady of patrician family, one Myrto, the great-granddaughter of Aristides the Just.[56]

The chronology of this second marriage is decidedly questionable. Aristides died a few years after the ostracism of Themistocles which occurred some time between 476-471. It would, therefore, not be far wrong to place the date of Aristides' death at about 470. Since he was 65 at the time he could hardly have been more than a very recent grandfather. Assuming this as a probable view, then Aristides' great-granddaughter, Myrto, could not have been of marriageable age before 425. Thus we may reasonably conclude that Socrates made his second marriage when he was in his late forties—sometime near or shortly after the production of the *Clouds*. But there is one serious difficulty involved in this view—namely, that Plato in the *Phaedo* (60A) represents Xanthippe as present in Socrates' prison cell after the trial. But as she is represented carrying a little child and as Socrates was 70 and Xanthippe must have been nearly as old, we are forced to a certain uneasiness about the literal veracity of Plato. The dramatic value of the scene, however, is great; Socrates' disregard for ordinary human family ties, his brutal dismissal of the lady, contrast vividly with his passion for transcendental notions and his tender caresses for the lovely locks of Phaedo.

Grant's view is worth quoting. 'Diogenes Laertius, Athenaeus, and Plutarch all state that Socrates was married twice. At the time of his death he had one grown-up son, Lamprocles, and two infants. The *Memorabilia* mentions a conversation with Lamprocles, who complained of his mother's temper, while Socrates good naturedly urged that it was of no consequence. But who was the mother of Lamprocles? Diogenes says that the two wives were Myrto (great-granddaughter of Aristides) and Xanthippe, but that it is doubtful which was the first wife. Evidently the first wife, the mother of Lamprocles, was the scold. Plato in the *Phaedo* definitely mentions Xanthippe as coming to the condemned cell of Socrates. This would make her the second wife. Equally definitely Xenophon in the *Banquet* mentions Xanthippe as married to Socrates, and as famous for her bad temper, twenty years before. This would probably make her the first wife. Between these two authorities the issue must lie. On the whole, in a matter of this kind it seems more likely that Plato made a slip. Xanthippe's name was perhaps so familiar as being the wife of Socrates that Plato forgot the second marriage with Myrto when introducing the wife in the death scene, at which he himself had not been present. Poor Xanthippe's tongue had probably been "stopped with dust" ere this scene occurred.'

The implications of this second marriage will be discussed in connection with Socrates' later life.

In the early part of his life, his interests were those of the democratic, radical, skeptical group, and his intellectual affinities were with the scientific materialists—the school of Anaxagoras (particularly as developed by Archelaus) and the radical social thinkers, the sophists. To this period of his life, too, belongs his association with Protagoras, the eminent sophist and the leading skeptical thinker. Plato describes their relationship as having been a friendly one and mentions Protagoras' opinion of the young Socrates to the effect that "he thought him the ablest man of his years that he had ever met and feels confident of his future." [57] It seems evident from the *Protagoras* that the relationship between them was not confined to the chance meeting at which the dialogue took place; the young student in the dialogue came to Socrates to get an introduction to Protagoras. The inference is that in the past Socrates had known the older man very well. According to two references in the Platonic dialogues he even seems to have attended the lectures of the famous sophist, Prodicus.

A passage in the *Meno* is very clear. Socrates complains that Gorgias had performed inadequately the education of the young Meno, and that Prodicus had not sufficiently educated him.[58] In the *Cratylus*, too, he mentions Prodicus as his teacher.[59] In the *Menexenus* Plato makes Socrates refer quite intimately to a long conversation with Aspasia and indicates that she had taught him literature.[60] In the same context Connus is mentioned as his instructor in rhetoric.[61] All in all there seems ample reason for connecting the early Socrates both with the sophistic movement and its leading personalities.

Two references to Prodicus in Aristophanes give us a strong hint of Prodicus' interests in cosmology and cosmological speculation. In the *Clouds* he is addressed by the sovereign and cloudy deities as the most pre-eminent of the "sky-way sophists" (*meteorosophistai*).[62] In the *Birds*, the promise is definitely given in the "Grand Chorus." [63] The *Birds* will instruct mortals in cosmology.

We will tell you of things transcendental: of Springs, and of Rivers, the mighty upheaval,
The nature of Birds; and the birth of the gods, and of Chaos and Darkness primaeval.
When this ye shall know, let old Prodicus go, and be hanged without hope of reprieval.

This burlesque of a semi-Orphic and mystical cosmogeny is set in sharp contrast to the "scientific" views of the sophist.

The *Birds* will thus give mortals the necessary information to refute the scientific theories of Prodicus. This does not bear out the theory of Burnet that the interests of the sophists were anti-scientific.

Of this period in the life of Socrates we can assume that the *Clouds* gives a true, if caricatured, picture. In fact only on such an assumption does the *Clouds* become a drama with any real content. As we mentioned before, Aristophanes intended his play, like all his plays, to be real social satire. As Taylor well argues, "The caricature must be or must be believed by the public to be, like its original. And the likeness must be such that there can be no possible doubt in the mind of the public as to the person aimed at." [64] The *Clouds* clearly is an attack by an essentially conservative playwright on the foremost and best-known exponents of popular materialism and radical skepticism at Athens. It is extremely significant that he picks out Socrates as the central figure for his derisive portrait of these tendencies. It means that Socrates had by this time attracted a great deal of attention and that Aristophanes' portrayal could be accepted by the public as characteristic of this group.

Now several points emerge into focus from the *Clouds* In the first place it appears that Socrates was poor and that his followers belonged to the poorer classes—were, in fact, slaves or artisans. We can conjecture that two associates mentioned only by Diogenes were among this group of followers There was Simon, a cobbler, who took notes on his leather materials, and, if we can judge from the titles of his dialogues preserved by Diogenes Laertius, [65] later followed Socrates into idealism. Then, too, there was a certain Phaedon, a man of noble family who had come to an unfortunate end and was now forcibly detained in a house of ill-fame. However, we are told he "used to close the door and so contrived to join Socrates' circle." [66]

In the second place, the nature of the intellectual interests of the school are quite clear from Aristophanes' buffoonery. The scholars were interested in scientific investigation and practical experimental science above all else. One of the high points in the drama is the remarkably clever description of the school's laboratory work. They measure the length of a flea's jump; they are eager to discover with which end of his anatomy a gnat makes a noise; Socrates is depicted in a basket observing heavenly phenomena. In reply to a question of Strepsiades, Socrates explains his

[66] Unhappily Diogenes does not state explicitly on which side of the door Socrates and his companions were to be found.

task: "I am treading on air and thinking my way 'round the sun.'"[67] The result of this sort of speculation is clearly atheistic; Zeus is banished and vortex is king.

Lastly Strepsiades is interested in Socrates' teaching as tending to logical skepticism (the famous *dissoi logoi*, or "two arguments") and practical citizenship, the clever conduct of one's own affairs in the law courts and in business. In this sense, he is the typical sophist.

Aristophanes' use of the two *logoi* in the *Clouds*[68] illustrates very clearly the clever way in which the idealists handled the position of the sophists in terms of the categories of their own thinking. The passage clearly refers to the famous "promise" of Protagoras to which Aristotle refers[69] that the sophists can make the weaker argument the stronger and can teach others who take their course in rhetoric to do the same thing. The meaning of this in the system of Protagoras should be quite clear. Protagoras, be it remembered, was a relativist. Individual man was the measure of all things, and it seems probable that he was primarily thinking in terms of ethics and political systems when he took this position. This is made quite apparent in the passage already quoted from Sextus Empiricus, the very fact that Protagoras does not transfer his concept of relativity to the physical world, but instead posits an objective substratum of material reality, shows that the emphasis in his thinking was on the problem of social relations. There is no absolute system of morality. Laws, constitutions and ethical precepts are a matter of "convention" and have no sanction in the innermost "nature" of things. In other words, we are dealing here, in another form, with the famous contribution of the sophists—the distinction between "nature" and "convention." But for the idealists and conservatives there was no such distinction; a system of justice and a code of laws are absolute and "just." Human nature and social law are related phases of the transcendent moral idea. This point is made exceptionally clear in Plato.

Since, therefore, the sophists held that there was nothing absolute or sanctified about a code of law or an ethical system, they considered it neither moral nor immoral for a man to use skillful and subtle argument in order to escape from the compulsions and possible penalties of an arbitrary custom. There is a close connection between the Protagorean statement that "man is the measure of all things," and the distinction made by the sophists between "nature" and "convention." Following their logic we can see their position as follows. since individual man is the criterion of any truth and it is only a truth in so far as he perceives it, there can be no universal morality above and beyond his own judgment. The state and its social laws that are forced on him he need not accept, for they are artificial regulations, valid only as "conventions," and are not "natural" laws. Similarly the absolute relativists, like Protagoras, did not condemn the existence of custom or man-made law as a violation of any *moral*-right, but simply adopted the position that no law can be universally binding for a whole society, since every individual is his own measuring-rod, his own determinant of right or wrong.

We have analyzed the implications of the sophistic point of view in order to demonstrate that it led to a final negation of morality and a skeptical, amoral relativism. In practice, the sophists utilized the art of rhetoric, and offered to train men in the science of debate. This, they maintained, was the simplest way to avoid legal "convention"; if a man were clever enough he could circumvent the law. This is also what Protagoras must have meant by "making the weaker [argument] the stronger." Translated literally the phrase means nothing more. It suggests a man with a weak case (perhaps a lawsuit) making it stronger and more effective.

It is important to see how Aristophanes, as a typical conservative and champion of the ethical absolutes, treats the sophistic point of view as it is expressed in the Protagorean statement of the "weaker" and "stronger" arguments. Aristophanes gives the thing an ethical twist by adding the phrase "more unjustly." He makes the "weaker" argument mean the morally baser and the "stronger" the morally nobler. Commentators and critics have tended to fall into the trap which Aristophanes and his idealist friends have set for them. They have failed to realize that Protagoras could not possibly have been using the words with any ethical or moral connotation, the only connotation is a legal one. Nevertheless, even to this day, there is a tendency to translate the phrase "make the weaker, the stronger argument" by some such equivalent as "make the *worse* appear the *better* cause (or reason)."

It is easy to see how the position of Protagoras led naturally to that of Thrasymachus. Protagoras had a concept of individual relativism; Thrasymachus of social relativism. In the first book of *The Republic* it is interesting to notice that the "weaker" is equated with the governed, the "stronger" with the ruler! The social implications of the argument become perfectly clear.[70]

For our purposes the main point is that Socrates is caricatured by Aristophanes as the typical Protagorean, as a master of the "two arguments," as the teacher who could enable men by verbal skill to evade the payment of their "just" debts. This is sufficient refutation of those who, like Taylor, strive to make of the early Socrates a Pythagorean.[71]

One other point in this passage is worth noticing. The young Phidippides is depicted as something of a social climber. But even at the urgent request of his father he refuses to enter the "thinking shop" of Socrates, on the ground that he would lose face with the Knights, or young men of the upper class. Here is another indication that Socrates' circle was not at that time as socially distinguished as it was in his later life. No young and aspiring social climber would hesitate to enter the circle of Alcibiades or Critias.

PART II

SOCRATES IN TRANSITION [1]

IN the period from 432 to 423 Socrates seems to have gone through the social and intellectual transition which marked the turning point of his life. Plato was certainly not wrong when he asserted that at some crucial point Socrates underwent a complete intellectual reorientation. But it is of the utmost importance to establish as nearly as possible the exact period when this transition took place. We have already discussed the inadequate character of Plato's presentation of the view that Socrates' thought entered an entirely new phase at an early period in his life. The fact that he associated with Archelaus brings this fact out very sharply and shows that the change must be referred to the time of Socrates' maturity, certainly at some time later than 430. By 416 we have a clearcut picture of the idealist Socrates, preserved in Plato's *Symposium* and Xenophon's duplicate work. We can only infer from the evidence that Socrates in 430 was taking a peculiar interest in the philosophies that grouped themselves around the figure of Anaxagoras. It is this period, 430 to 416, which must be considered as containing the explanation for this remarkable change both of thought and personality. The period is marked in Socrates' life by an increasing material prosperity. It is fairly certain that at the battle of Delium in 424, he served in a hoplite regiment along with Alcibiades and membership in this census was limited to the three wealthiest orders in the state.[2] It is even possible that during his earlier military service at Potidaea (432-429) he belonged to the hoplite rank. In any case this social position is far beyond anything which the earlier slave or artisan stonecutter might have enjoyed.

The period under review seems to have been marked by a steady increase in wealth. Putting together two bits of evidence from Diogenes, it seems very probable that Socrates at this period was independently wealthier than at any other time in his life. "Aristoxenus, the son of Spintharus, says that he *also* made money [i.e., as well as being a philosopher and discoursing on the conduct of life], he would *at all events* invest sums of money, collect the interest accruing, and then when this was expended, put out the principle again." [3]

"Again when Charmides offered him some slaves, in order that he might derive an income from them, he declined the offer and some even say that he resisted the charms of Alcibiades." [4]

The difficulty in utilizing the material of Diogenes is that there are no chronological indications. It seems to us, however, a probable conjecture that the first reference here quoted points to Socrates' participation in usurious activities in the period from 424-415, Plutarch tells us that Socrates lost 80 minas in speculation,[5] and it is tempting to connect this with the financial disaster that followed the Sicilian expedition. It may be that at this juncture Charmides offered to come to his rescue with the loan of a number of slaves. This would fit what we know of the age and chronology of Charmides.

This period of financial independence and respectable social position is also the period when Socrates "steered a middle course" politically and intellectually.

In the early years of the Peloponnesian War, the balance of political forces was somewhat as follows: On the extreme right was the oligarchical faction, in these years impotent since the banishment of Thucydides, son of Melesias (443). With this group there is connected, as we shall later show, the "underground" Pythagorean sects. At the far left is the ultra-imperialistic wing led by the extreme democrats, Cleon and later Hyperbolus. With this group we may associate the more radical philosophies of critical sophism, best represented by Prodicus, Archelaus, and Protagoras. Between these two extremes is the large and powerful group led and controlled by the Olympian figure of Pericles. This party is not, like the groups of the extreme right and extreme left, a homogeneous organization. It embraces several shades and tones of thought—from that of the liberal patrician, typified by the Alcmaeonids, who were land-owners, it is true, but had in addition important financial interests which were tied up with the advance of imperialism, to that of the businessmen and entrepreneurs, factory owners and free artisans. Of this latter group Thucydides may be taken as a fairly typical example. he respects Pericles, hates Cleon, and has for Nicias a faintly patronizing contempt. He approves of democracy in moderation but sternly opposes it whenever it departs from tradition. It is this moderate group upon which we must focus our attention.

For a whole decade the life and associations of Socrates were closely bound up with this faction. He was probably introduced to Pericles a few years before the war. He became an intimate of Aspasia[6] and one of that brilliant circle which included Phidias and Anaxagoras, a host of the younger intellectuals, and such a figure as Callias, the wealthiest Athenian of his day. The house of Aspasia provided a natural gathering ground for the culture, the charm, the talent and wit of the pre-war era in Athens. Anaxagoras set the natural philosophical direction for most of these people.

In this lively and spirited circle, the many intellectual currents of the day must have found a meeting place and a group that was sensitively responsive to various shades of conflicting opinion. But as the issues of Athenian politics began to sharpen and began to impinge with varying impact upon this circle, its members began to move in different, even opposite, directions. Some individuals, like the brilliant careerist, Alcibiades, embraced in one person and one career these opposite tendencies. Alcibiades began life as an aristocrat and tried to get himself named *proxenus* (or representative) of Sparta at Athens.[7] Failing in this he attached himself to the democratic cause and even out-demagogued Cleon in pushing forward the Sicilian expedition. Then the attack on him for the affair of the Hermes carried with it the imputation that his affiliations at Athens had not been entirely democratic.[8] Whereupon Alcibiades went over entirely to the oligarchical side and defended himself at Sparta in language that was blunt to the point of impertinence.[9] But by far the majority of this circle, as the war proceeded and the conflicts within Athenian politics became more and more bitter, found it advantageous to ally themselves with the oligarchical faction. Most of them were men of property; they represented the substantial elements in Pericles' support, the liberal patrician and successful artisan. But as the left went more and more "radical" in its treatment of domestic problems, the group came to find the program of the conservatives more and more attractive. For example, we find that Hagnon, who, when Pericles was accused of peculation, devised an ingenious political maneuver in his favor,[10] was one of those prominently implicated in the counter-revolution of the 400.[11]

We find some difficulty in accepting the traditional interpretation that the move of Hagnon, when Pericles was impeached, was directed against Pericles. The effect of his proposals was to modify the decree of Dracontides, eliminating the religious implications, ensuring a trial before a large popular court, and keeping the traditional method of anonymous voting by means of pebbles.

Few demonstrated the talent of Alcibiades for agile maneuvering. Most moved steadily towards the right. Socrates must have been affected by this process. Indeed, the problem must have been for him particularly acute, for Archelaus, the philosopher with whom he was associated, was moving in the other direction, dropping the idealistic aspects of the philosophy of Anaxagoras and taking more and more a thoroughly materialistic position. It is in this context that we can re-examine the relation of Socrates to the philosophy of Anaxagoras—the process as described in the *Phaedo* He became, so he himself tells us, more and more dissatisfied with the use that Anaxagoras made of "mind." Instead of a supreme teleological principle which should explain what is, in terms of what ought to be, Anaxagoras had treated mind as simply an element in a mechanically causative sequence.

At some time during this period of hesitation, compromise and intellectual incubation, he found himself heavily under attack by the comic poets and particularly by Aristophanes. The *Clouds* was produced in 423; it represented the counterattack of the conservatives on radical and skeptical ways of thought. It may even have been intended to complete the process of Socrates' conversion by holding up to ridicule the associates and modes of thought of his past. That Socrates was not insensitive to the criticism of the comic poets, he himself makes clear. In the tradition preserved by Diogenes, he said· "We ought to be particularly receptive to the criticism of the comic poets, for if they say anything that really applies to us, they will correct us. If not, they mean nothing to us." [12] What is at least certain is that the process of conversion was effective. By the date of the *Symposium* (416 or 415) Socrates and Aristophanes were on the best of terms, so much so that scholars since have refused to take seriously the earlier criticism of Socrates made by the comic poet, and in so doing they transform biting social satire into a harmless piece of horseplay.

PART III

THE LATER SOCRATES

WE now come to the Socrates of the Platonic dialogues, of the *Symposia*, both of Xenophon and Plato, the gadfly of the Athenian democracy, the scourge of statesmen, artisans and sophists. We can discern a great deal, both what is explicitly stated by his apologists and what is written between the lines—for silence is sometimes eloquent—about his private life. We find, for example, that the Socrates of the *Symposium* moves in very good society. He comes to the banquet from the bath, adorned like a bridegroom, and wearing sandals.[1]

There is the charming passage in the *Symposium* describing how Socrates is accosted by a friend who twits him on his appearance (the contretemps is described by a third person). 'He said that he met Socrates fresh from the bath and sandaled and as the sight of sandals was unusual he asked him whither he was going that he had been converted into such a beau.'

On the whole there has been far too much enthusiasm wasted, we feel, on the ascetic Socrates, the philosopher who scorns all mundane interests and turns in contempt from the things of the flesh. The episode which Xenophon relates, of his conversation with the lovely courtesan, Theodoté, indicates that the body even in his riper years was not entirely sublimated. The advice that he lavishes on an aspiring young lady of her profession reflects a warm and lively interest in quite unspiritual pursuits.

So far as we know, no critics have ever noticed the exquisite humor of Aristophanes' reference to Socrates in the *Birds* (1553).

The *Birds*, be it remembered, was produced in 414, a year or so after the dramatic date of the *Symposium*. Socrates' new-found cleanliness was evidently a subject for widespread comment. So, too, was his new interest in "souls." The temptation was too much for Aristophanes, his restless, devastating humor pounced on the situation and twisted it into a mocking burlesque. Socrates is so entranced with his new "mission" as a "leader of souls" that he has quite lapsed from his new-found cleanliness. The notion of this recent convert to elegance paddling around the marshes "unwashed" must have been irresistibly comical to an Athenian audience![2] He is now the friend of Alcibiades, Critias, Aristophanes, and Crito, and is close to the family of the great Aristides. At this period, if the tradition of later writers has any value, he marries into a great and proud patrician family. His wife is Myrto of the family of Aristides. At one point in the middle of his life he must have been moderately well off, but now he is said to have lost money—eighty minas in speculation.[3]

Plutarch has preserved two very interesting comments on Socrates' financial status. One was made by Demetrius of Phalerum who said that Socrates possessed seventy minas, held for him by Crito. The other, which strikes a provocative note, comes to us by way of Libanus who contends that Socrates had lost eighty minas in speculation.

It is tempting to connect this with the financial debacle that followed on the heels of the disastrous Sicilian expedition. We know also that one of his wealthy young friends—Charmides —offered to transfer to him title to a number of slaves in order that he might derive an income from their labor.[4] This offer he refused. (There is a lurking trace of irony in Diogenes' account of the refusal; in the same sentence he says that some even suggest Socrates was able to resist the charms of Alcibiades.) The refusal itself is unimportant. What is significant to notice is the relationship that is being formed between Socrates and his new disciples of the nobility. There is no need to press too literally the tradition preserved by Porphyry,[5] who is after all a very late and therefore unreliable authority, that Socrates profited financially from a too close intimacy with his followers. That such an intimacy existed not even Plato thought it necessary to conceal. Some of Plato's revelations are surprisingly candid.[6] While we must suspend judgment on the more immediate monetary aspects of this relationship, it is clear that Socrates was able to depend in any emergency on the generosity of his friends. In *The Republic*, for instance, when Thrasymachus demands payment for his instruction—payment which Socrates obviously is unable to afford on his own account—the young hearers display an instantaneous willingness to assist.[7]

Following the lively interchange with Thrasymachus—when the latter demands pay for his instructive discourse—Socrates protests that he has no money, whereupon Glaucon offers to come to his rescue and says that all his friends will chip in for Socrates.

When, after his conviction, Socrates is languishing in prison, Crito offers to pay the fine for him and enable him to escape. He says at the same time that there are several others of his young friends who would be only too happy to help save him.[8]

There is a clash of themes here, a contrast between the earlier and later figures of Socrates. Until the fatal transition his strongest characteristic is a kind of rugged honesty, an independence which is symbolized in his willingness to endure and even overlook the deprivations of poverty; his intense ardor to wrestle with the serious problems of physical philosophy in a tumbled-down, struggling school such as Aristophanes described. We can find far less to admire in the rather pathetic figure of later days—the Socrates who has lost all but the shreds of this dignity. The price he paid for well-being and the flattering approval of the nobility was a complete sacrifice of his own independence. From the moment that he yielded to the temptations of the "good and true" he became their puppet and apologist and was forced into a position of moral and financial dependence. The semi-religious asceticism and half-wistful mendicancy which set the tone of our later Socrates look oddly incongruous against the background of his earlier skepticism and the rugged, if honest, poverty of his artisan past. Perhaps even he was in some way conscious of this enormous inconsistency; we might read into his growing conviction that the truly philosophic mind is always independent of trivialities, a rationalization of his own abject dependence.

From Plato's main dialogues dealing with this period—the *Symposium, Phaedo,* and *The Republic*—we get a complete enough picture of the select circle who gathered round the master and participated in the discussions on philosophy. Among the better-known figures was Alcibiades, whose erratic career we have already mentioned. In his mature life he showed a strong tendency to embrace the oligarchical position. We also find Aristophanes, Socrates' old adversary with whom a truce had now been concluded on the basis of unconditional surrender, Crito and Critias, ardent and wealthy young patricians, one of them a stalwart supporter of Socrates at the trial, the other an all too-prominent leader of the reactionary conspiracy of the Thirty, Cephalus—the wealthy manufacturer who owned a large shield factory at the Piraeus—a Periclean democrat whose thoughts began to center on the eternal at the first prickings of a guilty conscience and whose politics became more and more conservative, became even reactionary, under aristocratic pressure during the period of crisis for the slave-owning democracy. Each member of this group in his own way, either political or intellectual, was bound up with the party of bitter opposition to the democracy.

A brief glance at a few of these personalities will afford us an insight into the essential character of the whole later Socratic group. Alcibiades was perfectly prepared to abandon not only democracy but Athens as well. He did both. Xenophon carried hatred of democracy to the point not merely of pamphleteering against democratic principles; he even deserted his native Attica for Cyrus and a Persian camp. Plato's loathing for the ways of democracy is sufficiently apparent in almost every line of *The Republic.* Critias is perhaps the most singular example to be found. He began life as a democrat and as a vigorous exponent of democratic thought. That he became the most bloodthirsty and reactionary of even the Thirty was in wide circles, and quite naturally, attributed to the influence of Socrates.

It is concerning this stage in Socrates' life that we find the most complete information, although it is refracted through the not altogether impartial eyes of Xenophon and Plato.

Two phases of Socrates' activity at this period are very striking. The first is the attitude he adopts towards typical representatives of the democracy. He is now represented as a kind of gadfly, pricking and tormenting artisans and statesmen, by showing them that their pretended wisdom is only a groping kind of trial and error. This is the period of ethical search for an ethical certainty, the attempt to find absolute and unvarying principles by which to explain all human action and to show the inner nature and essential character of such virtues as justice, courage, temperance and the like. This is the period, too, when there develops the sharp, unmediated distinction between knowledge and ignorance with the corollary doctrine that any action or belief which is not founded on "knowledge" of the essence of each virtue is to be regarded as useless and unsatisfying. In this, the account given by Plato in the Socratic dialogues and the picture drawn by Xenophon in the *Memorabilia* completely agree, although Plato has a much clearer notion of the implications of this view. In setting out on the path of philosophy, Plato builds on the teachings of this period of Socrates' life. The early Plato developed his thinking from a purely Socratic position. But a fact which has never been given sufficient emphasis is this that Plato could only have known the later Socrates. He was born, so Diogenes tells us,[9] in the year that Pericles died. He could hardly have been old enough to take an interest in philosophical questions until about 409 B C. By this time, as we have seen, the conversion of Socrates was complete and no trace remained of his past except a vague reference to his disillusionment with materialism. The loving care which Plato put into the dialogues is a most compelling indication of Plato's complete absorption in the figure of the master. He has neither wish nor ability to think back to the bad old days when Socrates dallied with cosmological investigation and sophistic arguments. He is fascinated by the overpowering attraction of the Socratic idealism and finds no desire for research into the less beautiful, less coherent, less reputable past. And so when confronted with the silence of Plato (and equally of Xenophon, a faint and muddled echo of Plato), it is important to notice that Plato could not have known the earlier Socrates and was temperamentally incapable of the effort of historical imagination required to reconstruct a youthful figure so altogether inconsonant with the figure of the master.

Now what was it that Plato and Xenophon found so impressive in the activities of Socrates? To the historian of philosophy looking at the period many centuries later, there is little implication either of profound hope or profound danger about Socrates' activity. Why should the questioning of representative democratic figures have seemed to the democrats so disturbing?

Surely it is not difficult to realize that this questioning was not merely goodhumored dialogue or an intellectual game, played *in vacuo,* but represented a positive attack on the most fundamental democratic assumption that politics and ethics should be the career of the average man. It made these primary social functions—ethics and politics—not the concern of *Everyman,* but the private preserve of a highly select, cultivated and articulate minority. In this respect it could only be called profoundly anti-democratic. We can well imagine that the very skill with which this confounding of the vulgar was carried out won the excited and enthusiastic plaudits of the young men of patrician circles, who for years had writhed helplessly under the galling necessity of political submission to men whom they regarded as their social inferiors. We can well imagine that well-bred but inarticulate young noblemen would welcome with warm, if clumsy, admiration this doughty champion, this Athenian St. George who so manfully lowered his lance to attack the "many-headed beast." We can equally well imagine that the process of questioning and confounding was an infuriating thing not only to the discomfited individual, but also to all those who clung to the democratic way of life. As the war progressed, as the struggle between the two

factions grew more bitter, as the democracy felt itself more and
more vulnerable, the role of Socrates, too, developed; from an
amiable, if somewhat irrelevant, nuisance he became a positive
menace. And so, in taking this argument out of the realm of
abstract discussion and drawing-room conversation, we begin to
re-create, at the same time, the clash of feeling and emotion and
begin to recapture some of the more vital personal and political
tensions that made the atmosphere surcharged with a sense of
crisis.

The second phase of Socrates' thinking and activity that clearly
appears is his affinity with certain Pythagorean thinkers and the
Pythagorean clubs. There is no need to repeat the evidence on
this point which Taylor has so well elaborated in his *Varia Socratica* But while we here pay tribute to Taylor for this valuable
insight, we must make one or two important amplifications and
criticisms. Taylor, we feel, is wrong in assuming that the Socrates
of the *Clouds* is already a Pythagorean. At the root of this notion
there is an irreconcilable contradiction, namely, the attempt to
bring together two inherently incompatible intellectual positions,
that of *askēsis* (or the Pythagorean doctrine of salvation) and
materialistic scientific investigation. While such an anomaly is
possible, even common, today, in Greece it was beyond even
the reach of imagination.

One of the most attractive aspects of the Greek genius is its
transparent consistency, its unity of thought and action, its profound sense for the essential oneness of all shades and aspects of
human activity. Society was less complex. it was easier to distinguish the springs that energized all activity. In fifth-century
Greece, when a man's politics changed, he altered his thinking.
And so, to a Greek of this period it would have been unthinkable
that one should devote one's life to an investigation of nature and
natural phenomena and at the same time turn away from nature
to a realm of pure and abstract form, denying to the body the
validity of its functioning. He would have regarded it as incompatible with the integrity that was born of integration. The Pythag-

oreans had an interest in science, it is true, but almost solely in the mathematical sciences and the logic of pure form.[10]

It is true that the Pythagoreans interested themselves to some extent in medicine. But it is very significant that their primary interest was in dietetics; and even here they never attempted to make a science of dietetics, but abstained from certain foods for reasons which science could hardly approve. Iamblichus gives us a fairly good account of Pythagorean medicine in Chapter XXIV of *Vita*. From this description it is fairly clear that medicine was rather unsystematically mixed up with magical and and semi-religious practices. They even cured certain diseases by incantation.

This kind of interest was not incompatible with a departure from materialism and scientific investigation.

Moreover, Taylor's concept of the sophistic movement is almost naively oversimplified. "In almost every point of importance the character ascribed to Socrates and his *mathétai* [pupils] throughout the play is ludicrously in contrast with all that we know of Protagoras, Prodicus, and their likes. They were *fashionable* men who moved in the *highest circles,* made large sums by their profession, and addressed themselves specially to the youth of the *wealthy and well-born class.** It was not the small farmers and shopkeepers who made up the *démos,* but the high-born and leisured *misodémoi* [haters of democracy] whose sons sought to buy the secret of success from Protagoras or Gorgias or Thrasymachus, and it is in this fact, as Plato plainly hints in the *Gorgias* and *Meno,* that we must look for the real cause of the unpopularity of 'sophists' with the *démos.*"[11] This betrays a failure to distinguish between the infinitely complex shades and differences of sophistic thought and their relation to the corresponding shades and differences within the democratic movement led by Pericles.

Taylor sees in general that the implications of Pythagoreanism are political. It is easy to discern the outlines of a very sharp antithesis between the struggles of the democracy and the semi-religious views of the Pythagorean school. The whole aim of demo-

* Emphasis ours.

cratic policy was the improvement in the material lot of the slave-owning democracy. Any improvement must be based on the destruction of the monopoly of the old land-holding aristocracy upon the organs of state power. As the effort to destroy the power of the oligarchs seemed more and more to promise success there came prominently forward a group of men, the Pythagoreans, who deprecated the whole struggle of material interests, who proclaimed the nothingness and unreality of the body and its material strivings, who argued that the body is the "tomb of the soul," and that the whole task of man in this life is to prepare himself for blessedness in the next. "In the *Gorgias*, in particular, this theory of the duty of man is made the ground for a severe indictment of one and all the famous men of the fifth century, who had created imperial Athens, and 'philosophy' and the *dēmos* are pitted against one another, like God and Mammon as masters whom no one can serve at once." [12] It is a pity that Taylor, who has seen so much, fails to see that the *dēmos* had an independent, philosophical position of its own. He fails, we believe, to understand the political significance of Thrasymachus and, in opposing Thrasymachus to Gorgias and Protagoras, paints the democracy as moved by a blind, brute aversion to all philosophical thinking, as purely Philistine, as a kind of collective "average, sensual man."

That the Pythagoreans were closely bound up with inter-civic and international reaction hardly needs demonstrating. This tradition goes back to Pythagoras himself. According to Diogenes Laertius he left Samos because of the "tyranny" [13] of Polycrates and migrated to Croton in Italy, where he established a constitution for the city and was esteemed along with his followers who were closely linked to the Three Hundred; they governed the city so well that it was almost an aristocracy. [14] Polybius describes a universal democratic revolt against the Pythagoreans throughout Magna Graecia. [15] Ritter and Preller comment on this passage,

[13] Throughout the sixth and fifth century in Greece, wherever we meet the word tyrant, we should usually understand "leader of the democratic movement."

"Causa erat quod Pythagorei cum optimatibus sentiebant eamque factionem sodaliciis suis maximopere firmabant."[16]

A similar picture is given by Iamblichus in his life of Pythagoras. In fact, the whole of Chapter XXXV is worth reading in this connection. The author, though he is a devout Pythagorean, makes no effort to conceal the fact of a bitter popular resentment against the Pythagoreans, and makes it perfectly clear that the struggle in Croton was a social and political uprising on the part of the democracy against an oligarchic clique. After the dispersal at Croton the Pythagoreans were scattered throughout the Greek world and took up residence wherever social conditions were such that they could expect a welcome for their doctrines. In the *Pythagorean Catalogue* [17] we read of cult members who settled at Metapontum, Elea (Parmenides, significantly enough, is mentioned as a Pythagorean), Tarentum, Leontini, Sybaris, Lochri, Rhezium, Selinus, Syracuse, Samos, Phlius, Catana, Corinth and Pontus. Iamblichus refers vaguely to greater numbers of Pythagoreans than the few he has mentioned. We know, too, that at Thebes and Megara there were strong outposts of the sect. Oddly enough there is only one name mentioned for Athens. This, however, is not so surprising even though it is extremely interesting. Iamblichus does not here mention the strong association made by the later philosophers between Platonism and the teachings of Pythagoras. Perhaps the connection was most closely perceived by Aristotle. Taylor has summarized Aristotle's comments quite adequately. "In the well-known chapter A6 of the *Metaphysics* Aristotle expressly begins his account of Platonism with the remark that it was much the same thing as Pythagoreanism with a few minor changes." It seems certain that Aristotle must have had in mind the development of Platonic idealism from Pythagorean speculation through the Socratic dialectic and system. In any case it is clear that our understanding of Aristotle's comparison depends on the recognition that Socrates supplied a link between Pythag-

[16] "The reason was that the Pythagoreans sympathized with the oligarchs and assisted this faction very markedly by their secret clubs."

oras and Plato. It would be beyond the scope of this book to discuss exhaustively the debt of Plato to the philosophy of Pythagoras, but surely this association does not have to be proved! [18] We could go on in great detail showing the philosophical connection between Pythagorean and Platonic thought. For our purposes four or five points are worth cursory mention. There is the notion of harmony (or as we should say integration) as the ethical ideal. As Plato puts it, "to become one out of many." There is the parallel notion of harmony as the political ideal—the subordination of all elements in the state to the ruling principle or class. There is the metaphysical concept of harmony and number as embodying the essence of things. And lastly there is the doctrine of the immortality of the soul and its imprisonment in the body, with all the ascetic implications of that assumption. For the purposes of this work it is enough to emphasize the direct connection. Socrates at the end of his life was a more or less orthodox Pythagorean. Members of the sect visited him in prison and offered to pay his ransom. It is to Thebes and Megara, strongholds politically and philosophically of the Pythagorean brotherhood, that he would have escaped, had he made the decision to escape and not faced death with resignation.

This very matter of resignation is important in this context. It ties in very well with the doctrine of the *"soma-sēma,"* the view that the life of the body is a hindrance to the pure and unsullied activity of the soul. Iamblichus (Chapter XXII, *V. P.*) says of Pythagoras, "If also, when he expected *according to appearances* [italics ours] to be put to death, he entirely despised this, and was not moved by the expectation of it, it is evident that he was perfectly free from the dread of death." The resemblance between this passage and the mood of the *Phaedo* and the *Apology* is so striking that it calls for no further comment. We might merely mention that all the Pythagoreans subscribed to this doctrine.

Now if we think back we are once again struck by the amazing contrast between this almost morbid welcome of death as a liberation, and the rugged self-assertiveness of the earlier materialistic Socrates, struggling to keep his school together and investigate the material causes of the things of this world. The Socrates of the *Clouds* does not regard the gnat's noise or the flea's jump as belonging to the dim world of appearance, or the vortex which banishes Zeus the king, or the *Clouds,* the sovereign mistresses that bring rain, the very essence of all that is. Again we may recall Xenophon's naive admission that Socrates' early interest in mathematics had been directed to grossly practical ends. This interest bears no relation whatsoever to the number mysticism of the Pythagoreans. It was an interest in functional mathematics, designed for surveying fields and contributing to the practical conduct of a life which to a Pythagorean was sick with the palsy of unreality.

Summarizing the results so far obtained we can begin to perceive the outlines of this particular pilgrim's progress. He appears to us first as a poor man reared under the aegis of Athens' greatest period. He launched his career as a thinker at a time when an artisan would not be despised by the leaders of the emergent democratic party. His early thought was closely related both intellectually and politically with the more vigorous and creative offshoots of this democratic movement, concretely with materialistic and skeptical sophism. Before he was 40, he had undoubtedly been recognized by the intellectual leaders of the age. We may remember the comment of Protagoras and his connection with Anaxagoras. This association with the intellectual and political leaders of the day brought with it attractive social opportunities, and in this period he seems to have held to the centrist position, wavering between the materialism of Archelaus and the nascent idealism that is already implicit in the philosophy of Anaxagoras—a range of thinking which corresponds to the shades of political opinion comprised within the Periclean democracy. As we follow him through the years of the Peloponnesian War we may observe the marked improvement in his material and social position. It is definite that by 424 he is a close friend of Alcibiades and is enrolled along with his friend in the hoplite census. Sometime between 423 (the production of the *Clouds*) and 415 (the *Symposium*) he finally resolves the conflict which has for a decade perplexed

his mind—whether he shall continue with Archelaus along the
lines of scientific research or follow the dissolving Periclean circle
as its most outstanding members are swept slowly but surely to
an alliance with the most unbending conservatives. As this conflict resolves itself, Socrates appears as a political conservative, a
friend of Alcibiades, Critias, and the other leaders of the discon-
tented nobility, and as a philosophical idealist, closely tied to the
Pythagorean school.

Socrates' later life is clouded by the growing suspicion of the
dēmos that he has been too closely implicated in the activities
of Alcibiades and his friends, activities which were highly treason-
able to the democracy, and which at this time foreshadowed the
conspiracies of 411 and 404. The notorious intimacy that had
bound Socrates and Alcibiades together since 424, or even earlier,
made it quite natural for Athenian citizens to suppose that Socrates might have had something to do with the peculiar behavior
of Alcibiades both before and during the Sicilian expedition. The
episode of the mutilation of the Hermes seems to have been an
incident fraught with historical meaning. It is too often interpreted
as the drunken prank of a number of young and fashionable intellectuals, released from every kind of religious allegiance or super-
stitious belief or from the simple faith of the vulgar, as a thoroughly irresponsible and playful deed. The known facts can be
just as well interpreted as a phase of the conflict between religions.
The known affinity of Socrates and his circle with the Pythagorean
sect makes the latter interpretation seem distinctly possible. Inci-
dentally the current interpretation of such incidents as this is still
too much under the influence of the nineteenth century, a period
in which the attacks of materialistic science caused all religions to
huddle together and treat each other with respect. A writer of the
Renaissance would have better understood that a conflict between
religions was a conflict between two ways of life, secular as well
as transcendent. The furious reaction of the democracy should
make us pause before we write the episode off as a capricious and
harmless schoolboy prank.

The years that succeeded the Sicilian expedition and its disastrous aftermath were marked by bitter political and social struggle in Athens. More than ever the oligarchical faction revealed its old and traditional willingness to compromise with Sparta as a way of fighting the democrats within. When the popular party endeavored to find a counterbalance by appealing to Persian satraps for assistance, the oligarchs felt strong enough to launch an anti-democratic counterattack. The failure of the Sicilian expedition had had the effect of alienating many followers of the democratic leaders, for there was a widespread feeling that democratic imperialism had overreached itself. The moderate party led by Theramenes put forward the watchword of the "ancestral constitution," the moderate democratic arrangements of Cleisthenes. Such an attempt to put back the historical clock of course could not succeed under the existing conditions of democratic imperialism. The more extreme faction of the right wanted to go even farther and undermine completely the position of the democracy. They were frustrated in this hope by a coalition between the party of Theramenes and the extreme democrats, the latter group rallying to the standard of the moderate party as the lesser evil. The period from 411 to 404 is one of sharp conflict. The net effect of the year 411 had been a modification of the democratic constitution, but the war still went on and the imperialists of the democratic party still hoped to recoup their losses. We hear little of Socrates during these exciting years but he must have followed the breathless career of his favorite, Alcibiades, with close attention. It was during this stormy period of reactionary conspiracy that the famous military trial of 406 took place, when, following the naval battle of Arginusae, ten generals of the Athenian fleet were accused of abandoning hundreds of their shipwrecked sailors without making any effort to rescue them. By an odd and lucky coincidence we find recorded in this instance the only directly political activity in which Socrates is known to have engaged; for just at this time he was serving his term as one of the *prytanes* (or board of chairmen).

The affair of the ten generals developed into a very serious issue when it became evident that popular feeling and indignation had risen to a high pitch. The *dēmos* thoroughly resented the undemocratic behavior of the generals, especially their indifference and disregard for the lives of hundreds of citizens. But more than that they must have seen in this event a dangerous kind of sabotage to the strength of the Athenian fleet. Athens, as is obvious, relied for her defense and the protection of her possessions on a large and well-equipped naval armament. Moreover, the sailors on the fleets (the "sea-going mob," the oligarchs called them) were the strongest element in the democratic force at Athens, and the fleet itself was the strongest defense of Athenian democratic institutions. This comes out most clearly in the account given by Thucydides (VIII 73 ff.) of the part played by the fleet at Samos during the counterrevolution of the "Four Hundred." The classic expression of their situation is given in the pseudo-Xenophontic *Constitution of the Athenians*. "First then I shall say this, that at Athens it is regarded as just for the poor and the people to have more [power] than the noble and the wealthy; and for this reason that it is the *dēmos* which mans the ships and gives power to the city. For the pilots and captains, the lieutenants, the lookout sailors and the ship-builders—these are the ones who guarantee power to the city, a great deal more so than the hoplites, the nobles and the aristocrats." [19]

Thus the unnecessary loss of hundreds of fighting men would be looked upon as a serious blow to Athenian defenses which had already been considerably weakened by the exhausting wars with Sicily and with her own Greek neighbors. It was also an extremely serious blow to Athenian democratic institutions and might be looked upon by the democrats as an ominous precedent if generals who too often betrayed the democracy were allowed to go unpunished after an act which was at best dangerous negligence and might be regarded as criminal sabotage. The anger and alarm of the *dēmos* undoubtedly arose as much from the realization that imperial and democratic Athens had lost some essential man power as from the personal tragedy of losing friends and relatives. We know that Theramenes personally conducted the prosecution and that Callixenus brought in a decree that the generals should be condemned by the assembly and put to death by a vote of the legislative body. It was this proposal that Socrates opposed, appealing to the *psephism* of Cannonus which provided a separate trial before the *dicasteria* (law court) in such cases.[20] This incident is usually interpreted as a proof of Socrates' high-mindedness and courage in opposing the irrational frenzy of the democratic mob. It can perhaps be better interpreted as a move in the incredibly complicated political game that was being played by both sides in this hectic period. It was clearly to the interest of the democracy to have the generals tried before a wider and more representative body. It was equally to the interest of the oligarchy to bring them before a smaller jury which would less definitely reflect the conscious democratic policy to arraign the generals in one block and fix them with a collective responsibility. The oligarchs would naturally oppose this on the sound political principle that it would be far less serious and incriminating for individuals to be condemned than for a group to be judged guilty of anti-democratic procedure, for a decision handed down against a clicque had unpleasant implications as far as the aristocratic *hetairiai* or conspiratorial clubs were concerned. The precedent to them might be highly dangerous. Viewed in this light it seems distinctly probable that Socrates was serving an essential oligarchic interest when he attempted to block the path of the democratic proposals. There is, perhaps, less a devotion to law and order or constitutionality in his action than a loyal piece of factional work.

The final years of Socrates' life witnessed several drastic changes in the internal and foreign situation of Athens. In 405 the Spartan fleet, under the efficient command of Lysander, succeeded in wiping out the Athenian naval force at the battle of Aegospotami. The results of this defeat were absolutely disastrous not only to Athens' imperial position, but to the actual independence and integrity of the city itself. Lysander proceeded to blockade the city and to cut off any possible assistance from the nearby islands which were friendly to the democracy. In Athens the political picture was turbulent and confusing. It was charged by the democratic leaders, and probably with some truth, that the fleet had been sold out by its admirals; that some of those in command had been acting in concert with Spartan policy. This accusation, for which there is abundant evidence,[21] sheds great light on the episode of the ten generals which had taken place only a year before. There must have been a deep-seated and not altogether unjustified suspicion on the part of the democracy that men elected to high office, at such a crisis as this, when divisions tended to follow class rather than civic lines, were not altogether to be trusted.

Now on the question of surrender to Sparta a very clear-cut division appeared in Athens. The traditionally pro-Spartan group, mainly oligarchical, favored surrender, and were able to convince many moderates that the position of Athens was hopeless. Against them the loyal, democratic and patriotic group held out for resistance to the end. At this critical juncture Theramenes executed a remarkable piece of political maneuvering. He offered to make a trip to Sparta, evidently posing as a more or less neutral figure, to determine the frame of mind of the Spartan ephors; to find out, as he affirmed, the best possible conditions for an Athenian capitulation. He remained at Sparta "as a companion of Lysander" for three whole months. "It seems to have been the object of Theramenes," says Grote, "by this long delay to wear out the patience of the Athenians, and to bring them into such a state of intolerable suffering that they would submit to any terms of peace which would only bring provisions into the town." [22] Theramenes accomplished his objective. After his return he was almost immediately sent back again to Sparta with instructions to negotiate with the ephors. The terms laid down by Sparta were uncompromising. Not only were the Athenian fortifications of the Piraeus to be destroyed, but arrangements were made by Lysander for the establishment of a thoroughgoing oligarchy.

At this crisis of Athenian and Hellenic affairs, Critias saw fit to return to Athens. Critias, be it remembered, was a pupil of Socrates and a relative of Plato. At one time he had been a young man of democratic sympathies, but unfortunately for his historical reputation, he had fallen under the influence of Socrates. Under his lead there was established in Athens the notorious and bloody reactionary dictatorship of the Thirty, comprising such moderates as Theramenes in the center, to Critias on the extreme right.

Critias stands condemned as the most bloody and vicious of this gang of terrorists. The terror was directed not only against democratic leaders but even against moderate oligarchs like Niceratus, son of Nicias, and wealthy metics such as Leon of Salamis. It was when the victims of this prosecution began to include even leading, if moderate, oligarchs, that Theramenes and other relatively mild conservatives began to suspect that all was not well. As often happens, political terror created a monster devouring its own children. Of these victims Theramenes is the most prominent. His characterization of Critias, in fact the whole speech given by Xenophon, is self-explanatory. "I agree with Critias, indeed, that whoever wishes to cut short your government, and strengthens those who conspire against you, deserves justly the severest punishment. But to whom does this charge best apply? To him, or to me? Look at the behavior of each of us, and then judge for yourselves. At first we were all agreed, so far as the condemnation of the known and obnoxious demagogues. But when Critias and his friends began to seize men of station and dignity, then it was that I began to oppose them. The man who gives you this advice, and gives it to you openly, is he a traitor—or is he not rather a genuine friend? It is you and your supporters, Critias, who by your murders and robberies strengthen the enemies of the government and betray your friends. Depend upon it, that Thrasybulus and Anytus are much better pleased with your policy than they would be with mine. You accuse me of having betrayed the Four Hundred; but I did not desert them until they were themselves on the point of betraying Athens to her enemies. You call me the 'Buskin,' as trying to fit both parties. But what am I to call you, who fit neither of them, who under the democracy were the most violent hater of the people—and who under the oligarchy have become equally violent as a hater of oligarchical merit? I am, and always have been, Critias, an enemy both to extreme democracy and to oligarchical tyranny. I desire to constitute our political community out of those who can serve it on horseback and with heavy armor;—I have proposed this once, and I still stand to it. I side neither with democracy nor despots, to the exclusion of the dignified citizens. Prove that I am now, or ever have been, guilty of such crime, and I shall confess myself deserving of ignominous death." [28]

Where was Socrates through all this? There can be little doubt that he was very intimate with the oligarchical leaders, many of whom he had instructed in the notion that only the good and the wise and the true should rule; that government was not an art that could be picked up at random by the "man in the street," but depended on "knowledge," knowledge of ultimate principles of the "good" and the "just,"—knowledge which could only be gained by study and a painful *askēsis* But it was not only on the theoretical plane that this intimacy existed. Two years earlier Socrates had shown himself willing to execute a practical political commission for his friends and his party. But now, in the moment of triumph and bloodshed and disgrace, the request came to him again. He was asked to constitute himself, with four others, a commission to arrest a prominent, wealthy metic, Leon of Salamis, and assist in the seizure of his property. This time he backed down. There can be no doubt that both intellectually and temperamentally he shrank from deeds of direct violence. It should be fairly certain that his sympathies at such a juncture were with the so-called moderates; with Theramenes and his sect, men who, in theory, were convinced oligarchs, who, in practice, were willing to intrigue with Sparta, overthrow the democracy, betray the state, destroy its fleet and, perhaps, regrettably enough, abandon hundreds of its finest sailors. But at the prospect of turning the terror against the wealthy and the prominent, these men drew back in horror. [28a] Neither Socrates nor, for that matter, Plato made any attempt to conceal their criticisms of Athenian democracy, its de-

[28a] That this is a fair picture of the feelings of Plato and his friend is quite definitely shown by an autobiographical passage in Plato's seventh Epistle. The high hopes with which they greeted the Thirty and their final disillusionment with the terror are clearly set forth. (324 b ff.)

pendence (as they thought) on the whim of the multitude and
the caprice of the lot,[24] nor did they conceal their preference for
Sparta's more aristocratic, oligarchic and servile organization of
society.[25] Moreover the essence of Socrates' teaching was, as we
have seen, profoundly anti-democratic, striking at the very theoretical roots on which the democratic way of life (even in a
slave-owning democracy) was founded. It is only when the logic
of political struggle produces a Critias, that such men as Theramenes and Socrates draw back in virtuous horror. However much
we may excuse Socrates from any responsibility or sanction of
the actual violence committed, we must nevertheless realize that
the instinct of the democracy was profoundly right when it saw
in him the evil genius behind the scene, the *fons et origo malorum;*
the intellectual center from which emanated the very heart and
soul of anti-democratic beliefs. We must here reflect once again
how closely philosophy was bound up with the factionalism of the
Greek states; and we need only recall once again the names of
Anaxagoras, Pythagoras and Aristotle.

Bearing this in mind, we are in a much better position to appre-
ciate the feelings of the men who came back from the Piraeus with
the experience of the terror fresh in their minds; and why, in
restoring democratic power, they should have felt it necessary
"to hew the head off and not hack the limbs."

Viewed from this point of view we read the *Apology* of Socrates in a very different light. We are so used to thinking of
the work as the high-minded *apologia* of the philosophic man,
remote from mundane things, high above politics and political
striving, that it is difficult to think of it as the extremely adroit
and facile plea of a partisan.

The setting of the trial, to begin with, was extremely interesting. The democracy, having restored itself and balanced the rather
precarious political position, felt it necessary to deal with the problem of Socrates. Three men came forward as his accusers. Meletus
for the poets, Anytus for the craftsmen and political leaders, and
Lycon for the rhetoricians. These three groups represent the intellectual as well as the practical leadership of the democracy. Sev-

eral facts about the trial are of great interest. There is no reason to think that Anytus—the central figure in the prosecution—was acting from any feeling of personal vindictiveness. We know that during the rule of the Thirty he had been forced to leave the city and that his property had been confiscated. Yet upon his return he distinguished himself by waiving any claims he might have made in the law courts.[26] As for the idea that the democrats were acting out of an irrational mania to pay back their enemies in kind, we have even the evidence of Plato to the contrary.[27] "Those who then came back conducted themselves very moderately." As a matter of fact the democracy was almost incredibly tolerant toward the men who attempted to destroy it. The only intelligible motive we can ascribe to the democrats arose out of a perfectly sober estimate of the danger both past and present represented by Socrates.

Fortunately we have two separate accounts of the indictment which check with each other admirably. Favorinus[28] quotes the actual charge as follows· "Socrates does wrong by not worshiping the gods which the city worships and introduces new deities. And he corrupts the youth." Plato's[29] version differs slightly but is substantially the same. "Socrates does wrong, in corrupting the youth and disbelieving in the gods that the city believes in, but [introduces] other gods."

We can only regret that so little may be regarded as established fact about the trial. It is even very doubtful whether Socrates made any defense at all. We are inclined to believe that Dr. H. Gomperz and Prof. W. A. Oldfather[30] have proved conclusively that he did not. Their arguments briefly summarized are as follows: In the *Gorgias,* Callicles draws a merciless if imaginary portrait of Socrates' utter helplessness when he will, some day, be brought to trial for his life. Socrates responds (somewhat later) by picturing the helplessness of Callicles before the Judge of the Dead, confused and bewildered, standing at a loss for what to say. "You there, exactly as I here."[31] In the *Thaeatetus* the same theme appears—the frustration and helplessness of the philosopher in court. Again the words, "all helplessness" (*pasan aporian*)![32] Then, by way of direct evidence, there is the explicit statement of Maximus of Tyre that Socrates gave no defense for himself, but that he "kept silence without faltering." To this Oldfather adds, "In the first place, there is an astonishing multiplicity of speeches ascribed to Socrates, or designed for Socrates, at the time of his trial, or composed in behalf of Socrates at some later date, by Plato, Xenophon [or pseudo-Xenophon], Lysias, Theodectes, Demetrius of Phalerum, Zeno of Sidon, Plutarch, Theo of Antioch, and even, seven hundred years too late, by Libanius." [33] The three speeches that have survived differ so widely both in content and manner that it is impossible to believe that they go back to one original. There are frequent references in Plato to the "ridiculous or pathetic figure which the philosopher cuts in the court room." [34]

The picture in the Platonic *Apology* of Socrates completely in command of the situation, exercising a quiet but compulsive mastery; the aloof, detached philosopher, the *aristo* scornfully mastering the noisy impulses of the *canaille,* contrasts very vividly with Diogenes' picture: "Justus of Tiberias in his book entitled *The Wreath* says that in the course of the trial, Plato mounted the platform and began: 'Though I am the youngest, men of Athens, of all who ever rose to address you,'—whereupon the judges shouted out, 'Get down, get down.'" [35] "The fact that Justus was a Jew," says Oldfather, "may not be regarded as quite sufficient to discredit his authority with others as readily as it does with J. Geffcken." [36] And it is no wonder that discipleship through the ages has preferred not to linger on or credit so unpleasant a picture.

Moreover, Plato's picture of the serene objectivity with which Socrates and the jurors discussed the fitting penalty, is turned by Diogenes into something like a riotous scene. The prosecutor had demanded the death penalty: Socrates proposed a trivial fine— 25 or 100 drachmas. The jury, a very large body in Athens, went wild Whereupon Socrates said that such a man as he should be pensioned for life. It is no wonder that in reply to such an impertinence as this, the death sentence was immediately passed. Eighty additional jurors apparently felt that the old man was incorrigible.

Around the figure of Socrates a veritable literary warfare developed. His friends and supporters poured forth a flood of argument, rhetoric, direct and indirect defense. As part of this systematic campaign, we can certainly include the *Gorgias* of Plato, the *Meno* of Plato, the *Apology* of Lysias, the *Memorabilia* of Xenophon, the *Apology* of Xenophon (or pseudo-Xenophon) as well as the famous Platonic *Apology*. Nor were his opponents silent, in the year 393 or shortly after, the sophist and pamphleteer Polycrates published an attack on Socrates which purported to convey the case for the prosecution at the trial.[87] The belief grew up in some quarters that this was the actual speech delivered by Anytus, but Favorinus pointed out, even in antiquity, that the mention of the walls built by Conon made this chronologically impossible.[88] The fact, however, that this particular identification breaks down does not invalidate the view that the pamphlet of Polycrates embodies substantially the actual case of the prosecution.

Socrates, then, within the space of a few years from the trial, had become a symbol around which the co-related intellectual and political battle of Athenian and Greek factions was raging. We are irresistibly reminded of the parallel with another philosopher who became embroiled deeply in the political life of a period of crisis—Cato Uticensis. As with Socrates, the battle of words and pamphlets raged as merrily around the memory of the dead Cato as ever the war of weapons had raged in his lifetime. But the attempt to build a *cultus* around Cato was not as markedly successful, perhaps because it faced the political as well as the literary opposition of Julius Caesar.

It is important to notice that the whole effort of the conservative faction was to lift Socrates above the struggle of contending factions and make him a symbol of certain eternal and absolute moral and religious ideas. The aim of the democrats, on the other hand, was to keep the argument on a strictly political level.[89] The conservatives were eager to take their philosopher from earth to heaven, the democrats were equally eager to pin him down to mother earth. In this way two distinct conceptions of Socrates developed. Out of the one evolved the figure of the symbolic Socrates—the mouthpiece of the eternal, the prophet who enunciates ideas of absolute and universal validity, principles of morality and justice which are to be regarded as always and everywhere true, without reference to time and space, out of the other, the lost Socrates, an historical personality, the intellectual leader of an Athenian faction, the man who more than any other was responsible, in an intellectual and moral sense, for the counterrevolution, and even (his opponents thought) for the excesses of the Thirty. And it is important to see that for the conservative intellectual position as Plato developed it, with its emphasis on the eternal idea, the claim of the state to autonomy and absolute obedience, the repudiation of the distinction between "nature" and "convention," the insistence that human law is the very incarnation of the eternal principle, the concept of the ethical and political ideal as unity and harmony, the submission of the passions to reason, the subordination of the governed to the governor, the "agreement" between classes that only the "guardians" must rule, for all this the figure of the symbolic Socrates was essential. Hence the eagerness of the Socratics to pitch the argument on an ethical, moral, religious and absolutist plane, to divorce Socrates from the struggle of factions and to make him a figure antipathetic to both sides. Xenophon, for example, does his best to make it appear that Critias and Socrates were at odds. He represents the decree passed by the Thirty against the sophists, forbidding men "to teach the art of words," [40] as a direct personal insult to Socrates himself. This is distinctly improbable, and it is a view which Xenophon himself refutes when he discloses the fact that in spite of the decree Socrates continued to teach the technique of interlocution.[41] The Thirty were not the kind of people to pass such a measure without intending its enforcement.[42]

This is not intended to deny the possibility that there may have been divergences of interest between the conservatives themselves. That there were such divergences is clear from the fate of Theramenes. Both factions, however, appealed to the concept of 'oligarchical merit.' When the right wing was for a short time in power these divergences broke out very violently and it is not at all impossible that the sympathies of Socrates were with Theramenes and the moderates rather than Critias and the extremists. That this is probable is shown by the critical language which even so convinced a right winger as Xenophon uses about Critias.

We cannot believe that the uncompromising terrorists, who were responsible for something like fifteen hundred political murders including that of Theramenes, would have hesitated to put the dissident philosopher out of the way.

It is with this divergence in aim and method in mind that we must examine the principal document on each side of the argument; the moving and eloquent apology which Plato puts into the mouth of Socrates on the one side, and the pamphlet of Polycrates on the other. As we examine the *Apology* certain things become very clear.

First and foremost, Socrates tells us, he is quite conscious that he is personally very unpopular in Athens, and that any defense he can make must begin with a frank discussion of the suspicion and slander that surround his name. It should be sufficiently clear, by now, on what the suspicion was based. Socrates, as Taylor very well sees, was suspected of being the head and center of an anti-democratic conspiratorial club. The youth whom he was accused of corrupting were wealthy and patrician young men, like Critias and Alcibiades, whom, it was thought, he had indoctrinated with his own contempt for democracy, his own esteem for oligarchical merit, his own conviction that only knowledge and wisdom entitled one to rule, his own suspicion that artisans and democratic statesmen could not possess this knowledge or wisdom, and his own doctrine that such wisdom was accessible only as a result of a semi-religious "search," of philosophy as a way of life. The new gods whom he was accused of introducing were the mystic divinities of Pythagorean sects—the militant protective deities of international conservatism. It should be clear, too, that this suspicion in the minds of Athenians could not have been of long standing. It could, in no case, have dated back earlier than about 415, and probably did not become acute until after 406. In the *Apology*, Socrates takes great pains to confuse the issue and to confound the recent suspicion with the earlier attack of Aristophanes. He goes to great lengths attempting to push the distrust back much earlier in time. Explaining how the suspicion has arisen he uses, with almost monotonous reiteration, such expressions as "long ago," "many years ago" and so on. The cumulative effect within only one page makes Socrates seem like an innocent man who *all through his life* has been the object of malicious slander.

He deliberately confounds two quite separate things, the accusations that Aristophanes had made against him—based on the intellectual interests of his early manhood—with the distrust that had arisen much later. He tries to make it appear that the earlier kind of slander had made him suspect in the eyes of the democracy. "But these are much more formidable, fellow citizens, those who have influenced *the* many of you [notice "*the* many," i.e. (a technical term), the democracy, not simply "many"] from childhood and persuaded you and accused me without a grain of truth in their accusation—that there is a certain Socrates, a wise man, who is a thinker about astronomical matter and has investigated everything beneath the earth and he makes the weaker argument, the stronger." [48] The words, "*sophos anēr* [wise-man]," should put us on our guard. There is a clear attempt to implicate himself with the sophistic tradition, and to suggest that this implication was the reason for his unpopularity with the *dēmos*. The two specific charges he outlines are that he is a materialistic investigator and that he practices the kind of subjective manipulation of concepts which was the stock-in-trade of the sophists. It should be obvious, however, that if this were the charge and this the slander, it would tend to make him unpopular among the oligarchs, but certainly not among the democrats. The fact that he associates all this attack with the comic poet Aristophanes should make the point and its implications perfectly clear. In other words, he was deliberately trying to confound the Pythagorean *askēsis* that the prosecution was charging against him, with the materialistic method and the technique of sophistic argument that he had abandoned years ago. He has done this with such success that the two things have remained confounded and all the labors of scholarship have not served to extricate them. We may remember how Xenophon strove to show that Socrates and Critias were at odds, thus disengaging Socrates from any one position. Similarly Plato tries to implicate Socrates with democratic and sophistic traditions just as much as with oligarchical principles. It need hardly be said that Plato is not trying to make a sophist of Socrates. His purpose is much more subtle. He is trying to dissipate the general conviction that Socrates had taken his stand with the oligarchs.

That this is not simply a hyper-ingenious interpretation, but necessary once one appreciates the political issues of the trial is well demonstrated by the account which Socrates gives of the "divine sign" and the unpopularity which arose therefrom. "You know, I think, Chairephon," he says; "he was a friend of mine from youth and a friend to your democratic party. He went into exile with you [democrats] and returned from exile with you." [44] "It was this individual," says Socrates in effect, "who with his usual impetuosity went off to Delphi and inquired of the god whether there was anywhere a wiser man than I. It was this individual and this episode which started me on my career of questioning to find whether any of our great and successful men really knew anything. It was a democrat who launched me on my career of anti-democratic philosophy.[44a] And so, out of deference to the god I went around questioning our distinguished statesmen and craftsmen to see if they knew anything—demonstrating to my own satisfaction that they did not. And it happened that young men followed me quite of their own accord—the sons of the wealthiest parents, for these had most time, and they liked to hear the great and near-great exposed and did the same thing in their fashion." The whole account is handled with profound skill. The original unpopularity was a result of my brush with

[44a] The aristocratic leanings of Delphic policy and teaching have been well studied by Mrs. Smertenko in the University of Oregon Studies.

your old enemy, the comic poet. I was attacked for materialistic
investigation and sophism just like the great democratic thinkers,
Anaxagoras and Euripides; it was a democrat who started me on
the "quest" which has done so much to ruin my reputation with
the democracy and it is the sheerest accident that only wealthy
young men have leisure to follow me and imitate.

The rest of the *Apology* is in the same way an essay in persua-
sion. In the indictment Socrates is accused of disloyalty to the
state religion, but in the defense he very adroitly changes the
sense of this indictment so that it appears that it is charged with
atheism. Now such an accusation would obviously be ridiculous,
and in Plato's version Socrates mockingly refutes it.

Plato has done his usual thorough job of making the opposition
obligingly stupid. Meletus is made to blunder into the ridiculous
error of arguing out the question in terms of whether Socrates
is an atheist. And obviously he was not! But notice how skillfully
his argument is offered. Any tinge of atheism would be connected
with materialistic philosophy, with the doctrines jibed at by
Aristophanes in the *Clouds,* the banishing of Zeus and the en-
throning of Vortex or materialistic law. This is again the same attempt to confuse the issue, by defending himself against charges
which might have had point in his earlier life, but which for the
last fifteen or twenty years could have had no meaning To the real
charge of subverting the state religion and bringing in Pythagorean divinities Socrates answers only with impressive silence.

In his essay on the *Impiety of Socrates,* A. E. Taylor has discussed the nature of the real charge, proving beyond question that
the accusation was based on Socrates' known affinity for the
Pythagorean sects. Taylor bases his exceedingly well-grounded
discussion on the main point that the democracy suspected
Socrates of being "the able and dangerous head of an anti-
democratic 'club.' " The main evidence for this Pythagorean affili-
ation can be summarized fairly briefly. In the first place there is
the unquestionable fact of a contact between Socrates and a number of men who can be directly linked to the Pythagorean cults.
Some of their names appear in the Platonic dialogues. Taylor

cites the following who are mentioned: Philolaus [45] (though not referred to by name), the famous Sicilian Pythagorean, Simmias and Cebes, pupils of Philolaus, who were residents of Thebes; Echecrates of Phlius, mentioned in Iamblichus' *Catalogue* of the Pythagoreans, Phaedo, a friendly acquaintance of the "club" at Phlius, and Euclides and Terpsion, the Eleatics from Megara. [46] Secondly, there is the highly suggestive account which Plato gives of the generosity and solicitude of Simmias and Cebes who brought a sum of money from Thebes to buy Socrates' release from prison. [47] There is also the interesting if casual comment made by Socrates in the *Phaedo* [48] that if he had decided to escape from Athens he would, of course, have gone to Megara or Thebes, both strongholds of Pythagorean activity.

Most extraordinary of all, however, is the way Socrates has met the charge that he had corrupted the youth. His argument, in essence, is this: "To corrupt means to make men worse: I have made these young men better. How, then, could I have corrupted them? I have taught them virtue and knowledge." The implication to the minds of his accusers he mentions not at all—that in making young men" better" he was also suggesting to them that the "best" should rule; or the further implication that in contrasting these better with the worse, in exposing the "ignorance" of artisans and statesmen, he was showing that they were unfit to hold office; or the much more serious implication that the logical outcome of this semi-mystical, half-fanatical Pythagorean creed upon the excitable minds of patrician young men in a period of bitter political strife was the formation of anti-democratic clubs and even, in one or two extreme cases, of anti-democratic terror. How simple the ruse would have seemed to the prosecution from the standpoint of practical politics.

The other side of the argument has been laboriously and ingeniously re-created by recent scholarship. It is a great pity from the point of view of historical objectivity that the friends and defenders of Socrates have had almost a monopoly on the literary evidence that has survived. We are reminded of another parallel. The very sharp criticisms which Celsus in his *True Word* leveled at the tradition of Jesus have survived only in the refutation of Origen. There is, however, one important difference. Where in the case of the argument against Celsus, the polemic is not delivered until the early part of the third century, in the case of Socrates the literary *cultus* was well on its way to formation within a decade of his death.

Putting together Xenophon's *Memorabilia* and Libanius' *Apology* it is entirely possible to make out the main lines of the political charges leveled against Socrates. They have been grouped by recent scholars under five heads.[49] The first was that Socrates had been the teacher of Alcibiades and Critias.

Xenophon quotes as one of the charges directed against him that he makes his associates disregard the existing laws.[50] He further notices the charge against Socrates that the effect of his teaching is to make young men despise the existing constitution and resort to violence,[51] even more specifically that the association of Critias and Alcibiades with Socrates was the source of untold mischief to the state.[52] He is accused also of stirring young men to enmity with their parents [53] and that he quoted lines from the poets and used these quotations in a subversive way.[54] Xenophon has a difficult task in correcting the very bad impression that such verses torn from their contexts must have had on people imbued with a passion for democratic liberty and equality. The first is from Hesiod, "No work is a disgrace, but idleness is a disgrace." Xenophon explains that "he was charged with explaining this line as an injunction to refrain from no work, dishonest or disgraceful, but to do anything for gain." [55] The other is from Homer's *Iliad*.[56]

"Whenever he found one that was a captain and a man of mark, he stood by his side, and restrained him with gentle words. 'Good Sir, it is not seemly to affright thee like a coward, but do thou sit thyself and make all thy folk sit down. . . .' But whatever man of the people he saw and found him shouting. Him he drove with his scepter and chid him with loud words: 'Good Sir, sit still and hearken to the words of others, that are thy betters: but thou art no warrior and a weakling, never reckoned whether in battle or in council.' " Perhaps Xenophon's fantastic piece of

exegesis is worth quoting, ". . . What he did say was that those
who render no service either by word or deed, who cannot help
army or city or the people itself in time of need, ought to be
stopped, even if they have riches in abundance,[57] above all if they
are insolent as well as inefficient." It is no wonder that simple people who lacked Xenophon's ingenuity and talent for scholarly discipleship took the quotation in its more obvious sense. Libanius
mentions Theognis and Pindar as other poets in whom Socrates
discovered apt malice.

Again, Libanius shows clearly that one of the charges brought
against Socrates by Polycrates was that he was a teacher of the
young oligarchs. We may quote the following passages. "For,"
says he (i.e., Polycrates), "he teaches people to perjure themselves." [58] "*Allusion visible à Alcibiade*," says Humbert. Precisely.
"If then Socrates taught people to perjure themselves and steal and
commit violence and do all the other things which Anytus
claims . . ." [59] Here again there is a reference to Alcibiades and
Critias. Libanius, however, is even more clear about what is
meant when he says that "as a teacher of evil deeds he [i.e.,
Polycrates] has no one he can mention except Alcibiades and
Critias." [60] That, we should think, would have been mention
enough. Libanius himself admits that Critias overthrew the
democracy.[61]

To make his point clear Polycrates had mentioned the great men
of old, Miltiades and Themistocles, who had not consorted with
the philosophers.[62] And to show his own political position Polycrates spoke in terms of warm praise of such democratic leaders
as Thrasybulus and Conon who had not been corrupted as
Alcibiades and Critias had.[63]

The second charge against Socrates was that his teaching tended
to encourage idleness and neglect of civic duties. "Socrates," the
first statement runs, "made people lazy." [64] This was met by the
rejoinder that Anytus thought that only the sycophants (i.e.,
professional accusers) were active.[65] Socrates is accused of failure
to address the assembly. Libanius puts the accusation in the following terms: "He does not speak from the tribune." "Yes," is the

reply, "like many Athenians, following the precedent given by Solon, since he did not have a temperament that enabled him to consort with the people, and yet he watched over many private citizens. But if he saw immature youths mounting to the platform, he seized them, he checked them, he would not let them bother themselves with the interests of the commonwealth. This was the peculiar feature of Socrates' method, as a result of which he rescued the city from inexperienced pilots." [66] The implication in the mind of the accuser is clear, that Socrates did not feel at home in a public assembly, but was much better adapted to secret intrigues, to committee meetings, to the conspiratorial clubs, and intimate discussions with the inner circle of disciples.

Included in the accusation is the assertion that Socrates took no part in commerce and mercantile life, that he was not "a merchant." [67] This whole paragraph we shall discuss a little later. In the meantime it is sufficient to point out the profound significance of this charge, in view of the political clash going on between the democratic mercantile class and the wealthy agrarian patricians.

It is no wonder, therefore, that the specific charge is made against him of training his associates in an anti-democratic direction and leading them to overthrow the democratic state. "Socrates *trains* the young men to attack the laws. [The Greek word *askei* is the verb corresponding to the noun *askēsis* which, as we have pointed out, is connected with the Pythagorean, part religious, part political, part "philosophical" way of life.] The constitution is in danger. Our philosopher creates men who are reckless and tyrannical, insufferable, despisers of the principle of equality. Shall we not check him? Shall we not expel him before those who are nurtured by him overthrow the power of the laws?" [68] "He hates the democracy and persuades his associates to mock at democracy." [69] "He reproaches our [democratic] customs [70] and his accuser has dared to call him a tyrant." [71]

The final charge against Socrates is that his influence tended to make young men despise their parents and compare them unfavorably with Socrates, that it made them impertinent to their elder brothers. [72] It seems impossible to associate this with any specific individuals or instances, though it is possible that the extraordinary deferential treatment of Cephelus at the beginning of *The Republic* is consciously intended by Plato to erase this impression.

These accusations all point to one thing, a conspiracy against the democratic constitution of Athens and an intellectual assault on the whole democratic way of life. We should remember, however, that if the argument of the prosecution seems less coherent than that of Plato, it is only because the case against Socrates has never come down to us in a unified form. Moreover, coming to us as it does from the refutations of Socrates' supporters, we must conjecture that the defense has dealt only with those items which they felt they could convincingly refute. It is almost certain that much of the evidence actually produced against the defendant, and perhaps even the most damaging evidence, was passed over in silence.

Let us remind ourselves once again that in Plato's own admission the restored democracy had conducted itself with great moderation and that a clear majority of the jury felt that the case had been amply proved. All this should make us very hesitant to accept the conventional explanation that a high-minded and guiltless philosopher fell an innocent victim to the excited and hysterical passions of a Philistine and ignorant mob, that an innocent and tolerant soul was sacrificed to the machinations of cynical politicians, to machinations that his gentle nature could never really comprehend.

Some of our readers may have been vaguely disturbed by a method of interpretation which correlates social and intellectual forces which on the surface may seem unrelated. We must emphasize that this correlation was very keenly present to the minds of men living in the early fourth century B C.—clearer to them than it could possibly have been again for many centuries. This is shown quite explicitly in a paragraph from Libanius,[78] where the accusation is leveled against Socrates that he does not take part in the life of commerce, that he is not a merchant. In great scorn the defense supposedly asks how he could be a better guide for youth if he were a merchant. The rest of the paragraph makes it clear that there is a very close association in Polycrates' mind between three separate arguments—the argument concerning the clash between the mercantile and the aristocratic way of life, the discussion of the relative merits of the Spartan and Athenian constitutions ("no philosopher grows in Spartan soil"), that is, between the democratic and oligarchic constitutions, and the philosophical argument between idealists and their opponents. It is no matter that Libanius quite misunderstands the charge and thinks that Socrates is being reproached for his poverty. The important point is that this identification of an argument on three levels with the clash between two ways of life, mercantile and aristocratic, could not be an importation from the fourth century A.D., for in this period the issues were very different. It must go back to Polycrates and is a convincing demonstration of the position that we have taken—that there was a transparent unity in fifth- and early fourth-century Athens between thought and life, between philosophy and social antagonisms.

In the tradition that grew around Socrates hostile social forces found unequal expression. As we have already mentioned, one side of the controversy has already perished; the other side has come to us refracted through the eyes of a man of transcendent genius, but a man whose sympathies are evident. Socrates had the good fortune to die just when the great tradition of idealistic philosophy was beginning to find articulate expression and a respectable technique of controversy; indeed, he contributed not a little to the process. It is no wonder, therefore, that Socrates was caught up in the process of transfiguration, that he shared the ascent of philosophy from earth to heaven, and that the Socratic myth which has dominated the imagination of the ages, has been given something like a universal sanction and an absolute validity. For the movement which creates idealistic philosophy is also, to a degree, a process of canonization.

FOOTNOTES

FOOTNOTE FOR FOREWORD

1. Sir Alexander Grant Bart, *Xenophon*. (Ancient Classics for English Readers), p. 100.

FOOTNOTES FOR PART I

1. Plato, *Apology*, 17 D He was approximately seventy at the time of the trial *Crito*, 52 E.
2 Plato, *Theaet*, 149 A.
3 Third century writer, Timon of Phlius, in a satiric poem speaks of Socrates as the son of a worker in stone.
4. Plut., *Pericles*, II.
5. *Life of Marcellus*, ch. 17, trans., Perrin, Loeb. Quoted by Farrington. *Science and Society*, Vol. 11, No. 4, p. 439
6. Paus I, 22, 8 IX, 36, Diog Laert., II, 19 Cf. also scholiast on Aristophanes' *Clouds*, 773
7 Plato, *Euthy.*, 11, B
8. A. E. Taylor, *Socrates*, p. 32.
9. *Ibid.*, p. 32.
10. Two passages from *The Republic* may be noted, 495D and 522B.
11. Taylor, *Socrates*, pp. 78-9.
12 Hesiod, *Works and Days*, 201-11.
13. Plut , *Solon*, I, 1.
14. Frag 2. (Teubner ed. trans., Freeman.)
15 Listed as frag 3 in the trans. of Freeman.
16. Diels *Vors.*[5] 12B1. Eng. trans. from Burnet's *Early Gk. Phil* , p. 54.
17 *Greek Philosophy Thales to Plato*. For this exposition Dinnik has for authority the explicit account of Diog. L., 9. 50, Sextus Emp., *Adv. Phys.* I, 216. Loeb edit.
18. Plato, *Rep* , 492 A ff Trans., Jowett.
19. *Gorgias*, 481 D ff.
20. *Gorgias*, 491 E ff.

21. *Phaedo,* 96A-100A. Trans., Jowett.
22. See Grundy's discussion, *Great Persian War,* pp. 166-170. Herod., VI, 124.
23. Plut , *Pericles,* 16.
24. II, 14.
25. *Socrates,* pp. 50, 51. Plut , *Pericles,* 8.
26. Diels, *op. cit.,* 59B17. Quoted by Burnet, *Early Greek Philosophy,*[2] p. 302.
27. Diels, *op. cit.,* 59B10.
28. Diels, *op. cit.,* 59B4.
29. Diels, *op. cit.,* 59B4, 151.
30. Diels, *op. cit.,* 59B8, 155 E.
31. Diels, *op cit.,* 59B20.
32. Burnet, *Early Greek Philosophy,*[2] p. 305
33. Ed. Bywater. Frag 62.
34 Diels, *op cit.,* 59B12.
35 Diels, *op. cit.,* 59B13.
36 Burnet, *Early Greek Philosophy*[2] (Nos. 12, 13, 14), pp. 301-2. Diels, *op. cit ,* 59B12, 13, 14.
37. *Phaedo,* 96A ff.
38 *Mem.,* I, 6-14.
39. *Ibid ,* IV, 7. 2-6.
40 *Ibid.,* I, 1. 12.
41. *Ibid.,* I, 1. 11.
42. *Ibid ,* IV, 7. 2-4.
43 *Socrates,* p. 56.
44. Theophrastus, *Phys. Opin.* fr. 4.
45 Aristoxenus, A. P. Mueller, *Frag Hist. Graec.* 25 (ii 280).
46 Hans Licht, *Sexual Life in Ancient Greece,* pp 453-4.
47. Diog Laert II, 16, 19-23, X, 12.
48. Diog. Laert , II, 16.
49. Origen, *Philos ,* 9
50. Stobaeus, *Eclog ,* I, 56
51 Ps -Plut , *de Plac. Phil ,* I, 3.
52 Ps -Plut , *Strom ,* frag 2, if this can be regarded as reliable authority. Quoted by Burnet, *Early Greek Philosophy,* p. 73.
53. Hippol, *Refut.,* 1, 9 [D 563, W 15]. Diels, *Vors.*[5] 60A4.
54. II, 16.
55. Diog. Laert., II, 19.

56. Aristot. ap. Diog. Laert. II, 26. *Phaedo*, 89A.
57. Plato, *Protag.*, 316E.
58. *Meno.*, 96D.
59. 384B.
60. Some scholars hold that he was hopelessly in love with Aspasia. See Ad. Schmidt *Perikles und Sein Zeitalter*.
61. *Menexenus*, 235 ff. The *Menexenus*, however, presents so many internal difficulties that we should not build too much upon this piece of evidence.
62. *Clouds*, 359-60.
63. *Birds*, 692. Trans., Rogers.
64. *Varia Socratica*, p. 131. Though Taylor, as we shall demonstrate further on, by trying to make the early Socrates into a Pythagorean, quite misinterprets the real intention of Aristophanes.
65. II, 122.
66. Diog. Laert., II, 105.
67. *Clouds*, 225, cf. 1503.
68. Aristophanes, *Clouds*, 882 ff.
69. Aristot., *Rhet.* II, 24. 1402A23.
70. *Rep.*, 342 D.
71. Burnet in his essay on *Socrates* in Hastings' Encyclopedia holds that in the Socrates of the *Clouds* there were mixed Ionian or scientific and Pythagorean tendencies.

FOOTNOTES FOR PART II

1. As long ago as 1811, F. A. Wolf in the introduction to his edition of the *Clouds* of Aristophanes put forward the view that there was an earlier materialistic Socrates who developed into the later idealist. In so doing he protests against the tendency to regard the career of a thinker as a work of art, from the beginning final and complete. "*Es ist ein sehr gewöhnlicher Irrthum wenn man in weiter Zeitferne ein Leben eines unermüdet fortstrebenden Wahrheitforschers wie ein schnell vollendetes Kunstwerk anzieht, und ihn in jeder Periode seiner Tätigkeit in guter Übereinstimmung mit sich selbst findet.*" Zeller's refutation, based on a few lines from Aristophanes' Frogs (1491 ff.), and the silence of Plato and Xenophon hardly touches Wolf's significant observation. We fail to see how any candid reader could regard this passage of The Frogs as a criticism of Socrates for materialistic think-

ing It might better be regarded as a criticism of his impracticality and verbalism, almost as a call to action There has been a tendency in recent years to take up again the thesis of Wolf. Mr W. D. Ross in his Presidential paper read before the Classical Association in 1933 (*Proceedings*, p 9), for example, speaks of the oracle as bringing to a head "a turning of interest from science to morality which was in any case taking place about this time in Socrates' mind "

2. Plato, *Symp*, 219E, *Apol.*, 28E.

3 Diog. Laert, II, 5, 20.

4 Diog Laert., II, 5, 31.

5. Plut, *Arist.*, I.

6. Plato, *Menex.*, 249D.

7. Thucy., V, 43, VI, 90, Isoc., XVI, 27-30. Cf Plut., *Alcib.*, XIV.

8 Thucy., VI, 28-29.

9 Thucy., VI, 89 ff.

10. Plut., *Peric*, 32.

11. Thucy., VIII, 1.

12. Diog Laert, II, 36.

FOOTNOTES FOR PART III

1. *Symp*, 174A Xen *Mem* 11 ff.

2. The difficulties into which critics have fallen by a neglect of simple chronology, is well illustrated by Prof Ferguson's attempt to use this reference in the *Birds* (414) as supplementary evidence for the Socrates of the *Clouds* (A. S Ferguson "The Impiety of Socrates " *Class. Quart*, 1913. Vol. 7, p. 160). He uses the two as though they were identical sources for the same period in Socrates' life.

3. Plut, *Arist.*, I.

4 Diog. Laert., II, 31.

5 Porphyry ap Theodoret. *Gr. Affect Cur*, XII, 174, cf. Diog. Laert., II, 20.

6 *Symp*, 177D 198D *Gorgias*, 481, Plut, *Alcib.*, I, Xen, *Mem.*, I, 9, III, 27, I, 3, 12

7 *Republic*, 337 D.

8 *Crito*, 45 A & B.

9 Diog Laert., III, 3

10. *Varia Socratica*, p. 10.

11. *Varia Socratica*, p. 133.

12. *Varia Socratica*, p. 17.

14. Diog. Laert, VIII, 3.

15 Polyb *Hist*, II, 39.

16. Ritter and Preller, p. 29.

17 Iamblichus, *Vita Pythagorica*, Chapter XXXVI.

18 A. E Taylor has made a number of illuminating suggestions in his *Varia Socratica*.

19 Ps -Xen, *Ath. Cons.*, II

20. All that we know of the *psephism* of Cannonus is a reference from Xenophon's *Hellenica*, I, vii, 20, 34 See the discussion by Mitchell and Caspari in their edition of Grote's *History of Greece*, p. 757, note 2.

21. Xen, *Hellen* II, 1, 32, Ps.-Lysias, *contra Alcib.*, A38, Pausanias, IV, 17, 2, X, 9, 5, Isoc, *ad Philip*. Or. V, 70. In Demosth., *de fals. legat.*, p 401C 57 we learn that the accusation in writing was preferred by the commander-in-chief, Conon, against a fellow officer, Adeimantus.

22. Grote, *History of Greece*, Mitchell and Caspari ed, ch. 35, p. 769.

23 Grote, *op. cit*, 778 Xen, *Hellen*. II, 3, 56.

24. Xen, *Mem.*, I, 2, 9, IV, 6, 12.

25 Xen, *Mem*, III, 5, 14, Plato, *Crit.*, 52E, *Prot*, 343C.

26. Isocrates, XVIII, 23

27. *Ep*, VII, 327B.

28 Diog Laert., II, 5, 40.

29. *Apology*, 24B

30. "Sokrates Haltung vor seinen Richtern," *Wiener Studien* 54, 1936, pp. 32-43. Oldfather, "Socrates in Court," *Classical Weekly*, April 25, 1938

31. *Gorgias*, 486 A, B.

32. *Theaet.*, 172C-175D.

33. *Op. cit*, p. 204.

34 Oldfather, *op. cit*, 205, Plato, *Gorgias*, 484 D, E ; 468 A-C, 521B-522E, *Theaet*, 172C-175D, *Rep*, 517 A & D, *Laches*, 196B.

35. Diog. Laert, II, 41.

36 *Op cit*, p. 209 Geffcken, "*Griechische Litteraturgeschichte*, II, (1934), p 7n38 and p. 35n73.

37. For Polycrates see Cobet, *Novae Lectiones*, Markowski, *de Libanio Socratis Defensore*, Breslau, 1910; Humbert, "Polycrates," *Revue de Philologie 1930-31*, pp. 20-77.

38. Diog. Laert., II, 39.

39. Cf. Humbert, "*tandis que dans la graphé de 399 les griefs étaient avant tout religieux et moraux, l'Accusation de Polycrates se place sur le terrain politique.*" *Op. cit.*, p. 27.

40. Xen., *Mem.*, I, 2, 31.

41. *Ibid*, IV, 4, 3.

42 *Ibid.*, I, 2, 32.

43. *Apology*, 18B.

44 *Apology*, 20E ff.

45. *Gorgias*, 493A, cf. *Phaedo*, 61B-62B.

46. As Taylor points out, the Eleatics were regarded as "heterodox" Pythagoreans. *Varia Socratica*, p. 18.

47. *Crito*, 45B.

48. *Phaedo*, 98E.

49 See Humbert, *op. cit*, 28 ff.

50. Xen., *Mem.*, I, 2, 9. (Trans, Marchant. Loeb Edition)

51. *Ibid*, I, 2, 9.

52 *Ibid.*, I, 2, 12.

53. *Ibid*, I, 2, 49.

54. *Ibid.*, I, 2, 56.

55. *Ibid.*, I, 2, 56

56 II, 188 Leaf Xen, *Mem*, I, 2.

57. Libanius, *Apol Soc.* (Teubner), No 62, p. 48, No. 87, p. 62; No. 88, p 63.

58. *Ibid*, No 109, p. 74.

59 *Ibid.*, No 112, p. 76.

60. *Ibid*, No 136, p. 90.

61 *Ibid*, No 148, p 99.

62 *Ibid.*, No 155, p. 104.

63. *Ibid*, No. 160, p. 106.

64. *Ibid.*, No. 132, p 88.

65. *Ibid.*, No. 133, p. 89.

66. *Ibid.*, No. 134, p. 89.

67. *Ibid*, No. 134, p. 89.

68. *Ibid.*, No. 38, p. 34.

69. *Ibid.*, No. 54, p 43.

70. *Ibid.*, No. 80, p. 58.

71. *Ibid.*, No. 162, p. 108.

72. *Ibid.*, No. 102, p. 70.

73. *Ibid.*, No. 134, p. 90.

BIBLIOGRAPHY

1. BIBLIOGRAPHY

Benn, A. W., *The Greek Philosophers*, London, 1882.

Bertram, C., *Der Sokrates des Xenophon und der des Aristophanes*, Magdeburg, 1865.

Burnet, J., *Early Greek Philosophy*, London, 1920.

Burnet, J, "Socrates," *Hasting's Encyclopedia of Religion and Ethics*, Edinburgh-New York, 1921.

Burnet, J., *Greek Philosophy, Thales to Plato*, London, 1914.

Burnet, J. (Ed.), *Phaedo*, Oxford, 1911.

Burnet, J., "The Socratic Doctrine of the Soul," *British Academy Proceedings, 1915-1916*.

Caird, E., *The Evolution of Theology in the Greek Philosophers*, Glasgow, 1923.

Cobet, K. G., *Novae Lectiones*, Lugduni Batavorum, 1858.

Delatte, A., *Essai sur la Politique Pythagoricienne*, Paris-Liége, 1922.

Delatte, A, *Études sur la Littérature Pythagoricienne*, Paris, 1915.

Diels, H., *Doxographoi Graeci*, Berlin, 1879.

Diels, H., *Fragmente der Vorsokratiker*, ed. 5, Berlin, 1934-1937.

Dinnik, M. A., *Outlines of the History of Classical Philosophy*, Moscow, 1936 (translation by H. Pilger).

Doring, A, *Die Lehre des Sokrates*, Munich, 1895

Doring, A., *Geschichte der griechischen Philosophie*, Leipzig, 1903.

Dupréel, E., *La Légende Socratique et les sources de Platon*, Brussels, 1922.

Farrington, B., "Prometheus Bound," *Science and Society*, Vol. 2, No. 4, 1938.

Ferguson, A. S., "The Impiety of Socrates," *Classical Quarterly*, Vol. 7, 1913.

Field, G. C., *Socrates and Plato*, London, 1913.

Freeman, K. N., *The Work and Life of Solon*, Cardiff, 1926.

J. Geffcken, *Griechische Litteraturgeschichte*, Vol. II, Heidelberg, 1934.

Geffcken, J., *Sokrates und das alte Christenthum*, Heidelberg, 1908

Glotz, G., *Ancient Greece at Work*, London-New York, 1926.

Godley, A. L, *Socrates and the Athenian Society in His Day*, London, 1896.

Gomperz, H., "Sokrates Haltung vor seinen Richtern," *Wiener Studien*, 54, 1936.

Gomperz, T., *Greek Thinkers*, translated by G G. Berry, London, 1901.

Grant, Sir A, Bart, *Xenophon*, Phila., 1871.

Grote, G, *A History of Greece*, Ed, J M. Mitchell and M. O B. Caspari, London, 1908.

Grundy, G B., *The Great Persian War*, New York, 1901.

Harnack, A., *Sokrates und die alte Kirche*, Giessen, 1901.

Humbert, J., "Le Pamphlet de Polycratès et le Gorgias de Platon," *Revue de Philologie*, 1931.

Joel, K, *Der echte und der xenophontische Sokrates*, Berlin, Vol. 1, 1893, Vol. 2, 1901.

Joel, K, *Geschichte der antiken Philosophie*, Tubingen, 1921.

Kralik, R, *Sokrates*, Vienna, 1899

Leonard, W. E., *Socrates, Master of Life*, Chicago, 1915.

Licht, H, *Sexual Life in Ancient Greece*, London, 1932.

Maier, H., *Sokrates, sein Werk und seine geschichtliche Stellung*, Tubingen, 1913.

Markowski, H, *De Libanio Socratis Defensore*, Breslau, 1910.

Mullachius, F. W., *Fragmenta Philosophorum Graecorum*, Paris, 1881.

Oldfather, W. A., "Socrates in Court," *Classical Weekly*, April 25, 1938.

Pohlmann, R., "Sokratische Studien," *Konigliche Bayerische Akademie der Wissenschaften, Philosophisch-Philogische und Historische Klasse, Sitzungsbericht*, Munich, 1906.

Richter, R. H. M, *Sokrates und die Sophisten*, Grosse Denker, Leipzig, 1911.

Ritter, H, and Preller, L., *Historia Philosophiae Graecae*, Leipzig, 1934.

Robin, L., *La Pensée Grecque*, Paris, 1923.

Rock, H., *Der unverfalschte Sokrates*, Innsbruck, 1903

Ross, W. D, "The Problem of Socrates," Presidential Address, *Classical Association Proceedings*, 1933.

Schmidt, W. A., *Das Perikleische Zeitalter*, Jena, Vol. 1, 1877, Vol 2, 1879.

Scoon, R, *Greek Philosophy Before Plato*, Princeton, 1928.

Smertenko, C. M., The political relations of the Delphic oracle. *University of Oregon Studies, Humanities Series*, Vol. I, 1935.

Smith, W. (Ed), *Dictionary of Greek and Roman Biography and Mythology*, Boston, 1849.

Taylor, A E., "Socrates," *Encyclopaedia Britannica*, 14th ed., 1936.

Taylor, A E, *Socrates*, New York, 1933.

Taylor, A. E., *Varia Socratica*, Oxford, 1911.

Wolf, F A. (Ed), *Nubes*, Nuremberg, 1811

Zeller, E, *Socrates and the Socratic Schools*, translated by O. J. Reichel, London, 1885.

AUTHORS

Aristophanes, *Clouds*.
Aristophanes, *Birds*.
Aristophanes, *Frogs*.
Aristotle, *Rhetoric*.
Aristotle, *Metaphysics*.
Diogenes Laertius, *Lives of the Philosophers*.
Iamblichus, *Life of Pythagoras*.
Libanius, *Apology of Socrates*.
Origen, *Philosophoumena*.
Pausanius, *Description of Greece*.
Plato, *Apology of Socrates*.
Plato, *Cratylus*.
Plato, *Crito*.
Plato, *Euthyphro*.
Plato, *Gorgias*.
Plato, *Laches*.
Plato, *Menexenus*.
Plato, *Meno*.
Plato, *Phaedo*.
Plato, *Phaedrus*.
Plato, *Protagoras*.
Plato, *Republic*.
Plato, *Symposium*.
Plato, *Theaetetus*.

Plutarch, *Alcibiades*.
Plutarch, *On the Pleasures of Philosophy*.
Plutarch, *Pericles*.
Plutarch, *Solon*.
Polybius, *History*.
Sextus Empiricus, *Outlines of Pyrrhonism*.
Stobaeus, *Ecloga*.
Theophrastus, *Opinions of the Physicists*.
Thucydides, *History*.
Pseudo-Xenophon, *Constitution of Athens*.
Xenophon, *Hellenica*.
Xenophon, *Memorabilia*.
Xenophon, *Symposium*.

CPSIA information can be obtained
at www.ICGtesting.com
Printed in the USA
BVHW081120240722
642887BV00013B/1357

9 781258 160579